Cambridge Primary
World English
Learner's Book 4

Gill Budgell

Series editor:
Melissa Bryant

HODDER
EDUCATION
AN HACHETTE UK COMPANY

Registered Cambridge International Schools benefit from high-quality programmes, assessments and a wide range of support so that teachers can effectively deliver Cambridge Primary. Visit www.cambridgeinternational.org/primary to find out more.

Third-party websites and resources referred to in this publication have not been endorsed by Cambridge Assessment International Education.

The audio files are free to download at: www.hoddereducation.com/cambridgeextras

Although every effort has been made to ensure that website addresses are correct at time of going to press, Hodder Education cannot be held responsible for the content of any website mentioned in this book. It is sometimes possible to find a relocated web page by typing in the address of the home page for a website in the URL window of your browser.

Hachette UK's policy is to use papers that are natural, renewable and recyclable products and made from wood grown in well-managed forests and other controlled sources. The logging and manufacturing processes are expected to conform to the environmental regulations of the country of origin.

Orders: please contact Hachette UK Distribution, Hely Hutchinson Centre, Milton Road, Didcot, Oxfordshire, OX11 7HH. Telephone: +44 (0)1235 827827. Email education@hachette.co.uk. Lines are open from 9 a.m. to 5 p.m., Monday to Saturday, with a 24-hour message answering service. You can also order through our website: www.hoddereducation.com

© Gill Budgell 2021

First published in 2021 by
Hodder Education
An Hachette UK Company
Carmelite House
50 Victoria Embankment
London EC4Y 0DZ

www.hoddereducation.com

Impression number   10 9 8 7 6 5 4 3 2 1
Year   2025 2024 2023 2022 2021

Cover by Lisa Hunt

Illustrations by Crazy Cat Designs, James Hearne and Vian Oelofsen

Typeset in FS Albert 15/17 by IO Publishing CC

Printed in Great Britain by Bell and Bain Ltd, Glasgow

A catalogue record for this title is available from the British Library.

ISBN 9781510467927

MIX
Paper from
responsible sources
FSC
www.fsc.org   FSC™ C104740

Contents

Welcome

How to use this book

Structure of the Learner's Book

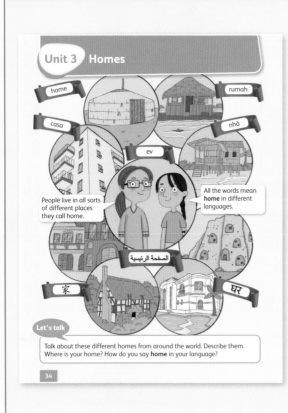

- This book is divided into themes and units.

- Each unit has an illustrated opening scene relating to the theme, followed by a speaking activity to guide you to talk about the picture and the topic.

- Each unit is divided into the following sections:
  - Listening and speaking (1)
  - Use of English (1)
  - Listening and speaking (2)
  - Use of English (2)
  - Reading
  - Writing.

- At the end of Units 3, 6 and 9, there are reviews to help you with revision.

At the end of the book, you will find:
- nine project pages with fun activities
- a glossary of all grammar points learnt
- a list of words used most often.

More digital resources are available as online resources from: boost-learning.com

Throughout the book, you will see these icons:

 indicates that there is an audio you can listen to. All audio files are free to download at www.hoddereducation.com/cambridgeextras

 tells you that the content is related to another subject you are learning.

Learn new language rules and skills with easy-to-understand examples.

Challenge yourself! activities make you think in different ways to further develop your English language skills.

Try this gives you fun games and things to do to actively practise and apply your language skills in interesting and unusual ways.

Do you remember? reminds you about concepts that you have already learnt about.

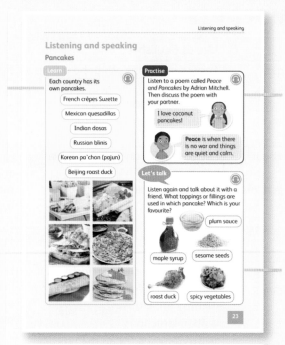

Practise new language skills you have learnt. Write any answers in your notebook.

Let's talk gives you practice in speaking and listening to English.

What can you do? lets you check your knowledge and understanding of the key concepts that you have learnt about.

Hints give you helpful tips on how to do things, and important points to remember. They also explain the meaning of difficult words.

Overview for teachers

Unit	Listening and speaking 1	Use of English 1	Listening and speaking 2
1	Locate countries on a world map Find out fun facts about Vietnam. Talk about own country.	Answer questions using the infinitive of purpose. Rewrite sentences using the infinitive or gerund verb form.	Identify missing words in a dialogue. Talk about rivers and what they are like.
2	Ask and answer questions about pancakes and fillings. Find out about and name pancakes from other countries.	Use countable and uncountable nouns with 'a', 'an' or 'some'. Offer things using 'would you like …'.	Find out about *dabbawalas* in India. Talk about a Street Food Market menu. Write about lunches at home and school.
3	Name different types of homes. Talk about homes and buildings. Listen to a poem.	Use imperatives to give instructions and commands. Identify imperatives. Write instructions.	Listen to a poem and follow instructions. Write and follow instructions to build a house.
4	Name objects found in space. Ask and answer questions about the sun and the moon. Talk about the sun, the moon and space.	Make sentences using the present continuous tense. Identify and write infinitive verb forms.	Listen to and research space explorers. Listen to and talk about an audio information text.
5	Name different musical instruments. Ask and answer questions. Match names with bands and musical instruments.	Use the present simple tense to talk about routines, habits and states. Talk about musical instruments using 'like',' love', 'prefer' and 'don't like' and the gerund verb form.	Match characters to their opinions. Share opinions using 'love it' and 'don't like it', and say why. Talk about music and music makers.
6	Talk about stories and story captions. Describe books without using titles. Make a bookmark to review a book.	Find subordinate clauses 'when', 'before' and 'after'. Retell and write stories using the past continuous tense.	Listen to and talk about stories. Join sentences with connectives. Order, retell and act out stories.
7	Ask and answer questions about robots. Read answers and ask questions.	Talk and write about plans using 'be going to'. Ask questions using 'going to'.	Ask and answer questions on a story. Listen to and talk about book blurbs and your choices.
8	Name different adventure activities. Ask and answer questions. Read and listen to a text and fill in missing words.	Ask and answer questions about activities using 'have you ever'. Write questions on a text with 'have you ever'.	Read and listen to a non-fiction story. Ask and answer questions about a story. Research more wild and funny stories online.
9	Name different school trips. Draw pictures of trips and write captions. Ask and answer questions on trips.	Use 'will' to talk about the future. Find future simple tense in a letter. Find examples of determiners 'each' and 'every'.	Listen to and read a poem 'The Owl and the Pussy-cat'. Answer questions on the poem. Give opinions about the poem.

Use of English 2	Reading	Writing
Use regular and irregular verbs. Rewrite sentences in the past simple tense. Use time connectives to join sentences.	Read and listen to diary entries from a story character. Answer questions about diary entries. Research a story.	Write a diary entry on a chosen picture. Practise handwriting by doing a writing test.
Use quantifiers 'few', 'a few', 'a little' and 'little' in sentences. Invite others to do things using 'would you like to …'.	Read and answer questions on a fiction text about an Ancient Roman banquet. Find out about how the Ancient Romans lived. Read and explore words in poems and stories.	Plan and write a story using connectives. Write and present a recipe. Use a checklist to check writing.
Complete sentences using prepositions 'into', 'in', 'out of', 'from' and 'towards'. Use question tags.	Read a fiction story and answer questions. Read and act out a story.	Write captions for pictures from a story. Ask and answer questions on a story. Write a new ending for a story.
Use 'have to' and 'don't have to' in sentences. Compare pictures using comparatives and superlatives.	Read a fiction text about the sun and the moon. Talk about folktales. Act out the sun and the moon story.	Write sentences to retell a story, using pictures as prompts. Listen to and follow instructions. Write sentences to retell a story.
Use 'which', 'that', 'where' and 'who' to add information and to write sentences. Compare two or more things using comparative and superlative adverbs.	Read and talk about a music festival poster. Read a review about a music festival. Work out meanings of words and phrases in a text.	Analyse poster information. Create a poster template with information needed. Make a poster. Write a festival review.
Draw and write about what things look like. Use 'had to' and 'didn't have to' in sentences.	Read an East African legend called 'Running Rhino'. Match words with their correct meanings. Create a film strip with pictures.	Write answers to questions on a story. Write captions for pictures in a film strip. Identify and write shortened animal names.
Complete sentences using 'something', 'anything' and 'nothing'. Talk about a robot competition.	Read and answer questions on a news report. Talk about the different features in a news report.	Use a checklist to find features in a news report. Write a news report using the correct features.
Talk about pictures using adverbs 'never', 'yet', 'already' and 'always'. Write sentences using adverbs.	Read a non-fiction poster about 50 different adventures. Match words and meanings. Find and read about specific adventures.	Make an adventure chart with pictures. Write a paragraph on a favourite adventure. Give feedback on a partner's paragraph. Use a writing checklist.
Use 'might', 'may' or 'could' in sentences. Read a poem and find the modal verb. Find rhyming words in a poem. Write a poem.	Read and answer questions about opinions. Match words and meanings. Support an opinion and share ideas.	Plan a trip giving reasons for visiting or not visiting a place. Make a poster to share your opinions. Use a checklist to check poster layout, as well as own spelling and handwriting.

Meet the children

I am Sanchia.

I am Pia.

We are sisters and we live in Santiago.

I am Guss.

I am Elok.

We are brother and sister, and we live in Bali.

Let's talk

Do you remember us from Stage 3? Talk about what you can remember.

Meet the new characters!

I am Banko and I am 11.

I am Jin and I am 8.

We are brothers and we live in Hanoi. That's in Vietnam!

Where in the world is Vietnam?

Bali is in Indonesia, which is also in Asia.

Vietnam is in Asia. Where is Bali?

Where is Santiago?

Santiago is in Chile, which is in South America.

> **Try this**
>
> Work with a partner. Take turns to describe a character and guess who it is. Close your books to make it more challenging!

This is a map of the world.

Hanoi is the capital of Vietnam.

We live in Hanoi.

Ho Chi Minh City is the largest city in Vietnam.

Let's talk

What is the name of your country? Where in the world is your country? What do you already know about different countries of the world?

Listening and speaking

A world map, a country map

Practise

Listen and point.   Say each city and country name. Point to the countries on the map of the world on page 10. Use the labels to help you.

- Dubai is a city in the United Arab Emirates.
- Bali is a city in Indonesia.
- Delhi is a city in India.
- Lagos is a city in Nigeria.
- Santiago is a city in Chile.

Let's talk

Work with a partner.

1 Find your country on a map of the world.

2 Draw the shape of your country. Draw special things about your country on its shape.

3 Present your map to the class. If you live in Vietnam, find some different things about your country to talk about.

Practise

Listen and point to each picture as Banko talks about Vietnam.

pagodas

temples

rice grower

Use of English

Infinitive of purpose

Learn

An **infinitive** is the verb form with **to** at the beginning. It can be used as the object of a sentence to talk about the purpose.

Infinitive	Example sentence	Infinitive as the object
to learn	I **was learning** Spanish.	I went to Spain **to learn** Spanish.
to enjoy	He **enjoyed** the sea.	He went to the beach **to enjoy** the sea.
to buy	She **bought** a sun hat.	She went to the shops **to buy** a sun hat.

Practise

Write sentences for these pictures.

Answer the question:
Why did they go?

They went to visit their family.

Try this

1 Say or sing this funny song.
2 Where is the infinitive?

A sailor went to sea, sea, sea

To see what he could see, see, see.

But all that he could see, see, see,

Was the bottom of the deep blue sea, sea, sea.

3 Repeat the song with a partner. Clap your hands together as you say each word.

Verbs with gerunds and infinitives

Do you remember?

Gerunds are verb forms used as nouns. We add **ing**.

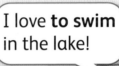
I love swimm**ing** in the lake!

We can use the past tense of the verb **to go** or **to do** to say what we did or where we went.

Pronouns	The verb	Verb + *ing* as the object
I/You/He/She/It	went	swimming.
We/You/They	did	sightseeing.
		sailing.

Gerunds are not the same as using the present or past continuous verb forms, for example:

I love **to swim** in the lake!

I am swimming.   I was swimming.

Sometimes we can also use the infinitive (to swim).

Practise

Listen to the sentences and write the verbs in two lists.

Infinitive: *to* + verbs	Gerund: verbs + *ing*

Practise

Rewrite each sentence using the infinitive or gerund verb form.

1 I liked sailing.

2 I like to visit other countries.

3 I love to travel.

4 I started to speak Vietnamese.

Hint

These verbs can use either verb form.

Listening and speaking

What's in a country?

Practise

Banko and Jin are watching a TV film about different countries.

1 Listen to them chatting. Write the missing words in your notebook.

2 Listen again and read it with your partner.

Banko: I like this programme, Jin. It's about different _____.

Jin: I wonder which _____ is the biggest?

Banko: It's Russia! But China has the most _____.

Jin: Oh… Oh look! That's a rainforest in the Amazon. It's in South America.

Banko: Yes, things like nuts and bananas grow in the _____.

Jin: I know that! We have rainforests in our country. We've got _____, rivers and _____ too. Some countries don't have that much water.

Banko: That's true. Did you _____ that we have a white sand desert too? And guess what?

Jin: What?

Banko: There are cows and not camels in that _____!

Jin: *[laughing]* Really?

Banko: Yes. The red desert in South Africa has red sand, but our desert in Vietnam has _____ sand.

Jin: And cows! I'd like to see the cows in the desert! I'm going to ask dad if we can go _____ _____ them.

Let's talk

Some countries have rivers.

Look at these aerial photographs and talk about these rivers.

Hint

An aerial photograph looks down on something because it is taken from above.

Nile River

Thames River

Kahayan River

Amazon River

1 Which country does the river start in?

2 Which sea does the river lead to?

Practise

1 Listen to this poem about a river. It tells us the river can be like people or animals.

2 What are the four things the river is like?

Challenge yourself!

Write what you think a river is like.

A river's a snake, stretching and coiling …

Use of English

Past simple tense

We **flew** to another country to see our cousins.

Do you remember?

We use the past simple tense to talk about something that happened. We add **ed** to regular verbs. Some verbs are irregular and we have to learn them.

Verb	Past simple tense	Sentence example
go	went	We **went** to the UK.
stay	stayed	We **stayed** in a hotel.

Practise

1 Listen and write the verbs in two lists: regular verbs and irregular verbs.

2 Write a sentence for two verbs in each list.

Practise

1 Read this text about travelling by plane.
2 Rewrite the sentences in the past simple tense.

Hint

Look out for regular and irregular verbs.

When we travel to another country, we go by plane. Travelling by plane is an exciting and fast way to travel.

First we check in. We show our tickets and give our bags to the person at the check-in desk.

We walk to Departures and, on the way, we have to go through security. Our bags go through a scanner and so do we!

Then we sit in Departures until we are asked to board. We keep looking at the flight screens to see where we need to be.

Finally, we board our plane and find our seats. The flight attendants make us feel very comfortable and off we go – it's take-off time!

Time connectives

Learn

We use **connectives** to join shorter sentences together. **Time connectives** tell us when something is happening or when it happened.

(before) (after) (then) (when)

Hint

The connective **when** means 'at a time' or 'during a time'.

Sentence 1	When?	Sentence 2	Sentence 3
We fastened our seat belts.	before	The plane took off.	We fastened our seat belts **before** the plane took off.
	after	We sat down.	We fastened our seat belts **after** we sat down.
	then	We waited to take off.	We fastened our seat belts **then** we waited to take off.
	when	We were told to.	We fastened our seat belts **when** we were told to.

Practise

Listen to and read the poem.

Find the time connectives.

In a plane
The ground recoils
    beneath us when we
    speed away from Earth.
Before we lift, there's a roar like a
    volcano or a hippo giving birth.
After take-off our silver stallion leaps
    the clouds and thunders
Towards the blue,
Then we gasp in wonder at the sight
    that opens to our view.

By Gill Budgell

Practise

Complete the sentences using time connectives.

1 Travellers can relax _____ the plane is in the air.

2 The air stewards serve drinks _____ serving a meal.

3 On a long trip, people sleep _____ they have eaten a meal.

4 The pilot tells everyone to prepare for landing _____ he lands the plane.

Reading

A diary

Practise

1 Read these diary entries. They tell the story of Robinson Crusoe, who was born in England and lived in Brazil, South America. He was ship-wrecked on a desert island for 27 years. He didn't know where he was or what country he was in.

Day 1: I am on my way to Africa, but I can see a dark storm is heading our way.

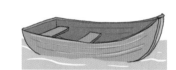

Day 16: Finally, the storm has stopped. We have been lashed by fierce wind and rain for two weeks. The waves rose higher than the ship and we did not know if we could survive.

Day 24: I only remember that my small boat was lifted up out of the water and then I felt sand under my hands and feet. I struggled to open my eyes, but when I did, I saw this empty beach. There are no people, no boats and no animals. There is sand, rocks and dense jungle. Where am I? What country am I in?

Day 20: The ship got stuck on rocks. This morning we climbed into our small rowing boats. We will row until we find land.

[A year later …]

Day 389: I have lost count of the days. I know I am on a small island in the middle of the sea. I have found fruit and vegetables growing and I have made friends with goats, chickens and birds.

Day 400: I am not alone! I have found a footprint in the sand There must be another human being here on the island …

2 Now listen to the diary entries.

Do you know?

Robinson Crusoe was written by Daniel Defoe in 1719. We think it is based on a true story of a Scottish sailor. There is an island in Chile that is now called Robinson Crusoe Island.

Robinson Crusoe Island, Chile

Practise

Finish each sentence and write it in your notebook.

1 This diary belongs to a man called …

2 He was on ship heading to …

3 His ship was hit by a …

4 After the storm, he woke up …

5 On the island, he found …

6 After a year, he was shocked to see …

7 It meant that …

Try this

Find out more about the story of Robinson Crusoe. Try to decide if you think the story is true or not. Find out how the story really ends.

Challenge yourself!

What happened next? Write the next entry that you think Robinson Crusoe wrote in his diary.

Writing

Write a diary entry

Practise

Imagine you visited a place in a country.

1 Look in some magazines or online. Collect some pictures of different countries. They can be real or pretend places.

2 Take it in turns to choose a picture. Write a list of things about the place. What was it called? What did you see? Did you know where you were?

I think I was in the Land of the Dinosaurs!
I could see huge trees and I heard loud roaring.
I had no idea what country I was in.

Practise

Write a diary entry like one of Robinson Crusoe's in your notebook. Use the picture you chose on page 20 and write in the past tense.

Day 1

I woke up early and looked for food.

I saw …

I ate …

Try this

Design a front cover for your own diary.

Challenge yourself!

1 Choose two sentences from your diary entry or from one of Robinson Crusoe's diary entries. How many times can you write the two sentences in one minute?

2 After the writing test, check your writing.

- Is it neat?
- Does it flow?
- Is it readable?

3 What can you improve in your handwriting? Ask a partner to tell you what they think.

What can you do?

Read and review what you can do.

✔ I can talk about my country and other countries.

✔ I can use past simple tense and time connectives.

✔ I can use infinitive verbs (**to + verb**) and gerunds (**verb + –ing**).

✔ I can read and write a diary.

Let's talk

What pancakes do you have in your country? How do you make them? Are they sweet like sugar or honey? Or are they savoury like salt or spice?

Listening and speaking

Pancakes

Learn

Each country has its own pancakes.

> French crêpes Suzette

> Mexican quesadillas

> Indian dosas

> Russian blinis

> Korean pa'chon (pajun)

> Beijing roast duck

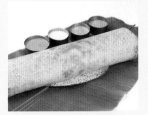

Practise

Listen to a poem called *Peace and Pancakes* by Adrian Mitchell. Then discuss the poem with your partner.

> I love coconut pancakes!

> **Peace** is when there is no war and things are quiet and calm.

Let's talk

Listen again and talk about it with a friend. What toppings or fillings are used in which pancake? Which is your favourite?

> plum sauce

> maple syrup

> sesame seeds

> roast duck

> spicy vegetables

23

Use of English

Countable and uncountable nouns

Hint

We also use **some** to talk about countable plurals.

Do you remember?

We use **a** or **an** to talk about singular things we can count. We call them countable nouns.

We use **some** to talk about things we cannot count. We call them uncountable nouns.

We need **a** large egg and **some** milk.

Practise

1 Read the recipe *How to make English pancakes*.
2 Find the countable and uncountable nouns in the recipe. Write the words with **a/an** or **some** in two lists.

Ingredients
- 1 cup plain flour
- 2 eggs
- A pinch of salt
- 1 cup milk
- 1 tablespoon vegetable oil
- Oil for frying

Things you need
- Mixing bowl
- Whisk/mixing spoon
- Frying pan
- Spatula to flip pancakes

What to do
1 Mix the flour and salt in the bowl.
2 Make a hole in the middle. Pour in the milk and eggs.
3 Mix together to make a smooth mixture.
4 Add the oil. Mix again.
5 Get a pan and pour in a small spoonful of oil.
6 **Ask an adult to help you!** Heat the frying pan.
7 Add a big spoonful of the mixture. Tip the pan so the mixture spreads.
8 Cook the pancake for about 30 seconds. Check that the pancake is golden-brown underneath.
9 Flip the pancake over and cook the other side.
10 Turn out onto a plate, and cook the rest of the pancakes in the same way.
11 Eat them with any topping you like.

Offering: *Would you like …?*

When we offer somebody something, we can say: **Would you like …?**

Would you like a pancake?

Would you like some honey?

Would you like some strawberries?

Practise

1 Listen to the conversation between Guss and Elok. Write the missing words in a list as you hear them.

2 Write out the complete sentences in your notebook. Draw the pancakes and fillings!

Guss: What are you ordering, Elok?

Elok: I'm ordering a _____ of course.

Guss: No, I mean what type of pancake?

Elok: Mmmmm … let me see.

Guss: _____ you like a thick pancake with some chocolate sprinkles? Or a green _____ pancake with a squirt of sugar syrup?

Elok: Mmmmm … Oh, I don't know.

Guss: Come on … you have to decide.

Elok: Okay, I'd like a thick pancake, please.

Guss: Would you _____ some chocolate sprinkles or _____ crushed peanuts?

Elok: Stop asking me so many questions! It takes time to choose the right pancake filling! [*Both children laugh*]

Let's talk

Work with a partner to offer each other these things. Say: **Would you like …?**

honey

strawberry jam

coconut

lemon slice

Listening and speaking

Lunch in India: *Dabbawalas*

Let's talk

Work with a partner. Take turns to ask and answer questions about this photograph.

Practise

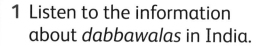
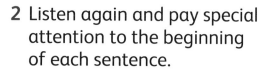

1 Listen to the information about *dabbawalas* in India.

2 Listen again and pay special attention to the beginning of each sentence.

3 Write the sentence starters in the correct order in your notebook.

a The lunches are made by …

b The lunches stay hot inside …

c This man is one of …

d On a hot Mumbai morning, you might be surprised to see a man wearing a …

Practise

Write the answers to these questions.

1 What is the bike loaded with?

2 What do *dabbawalas* do?

3 How many *dabbawalas* are there in Mumbai?

4 Who makes the lunches?

5 How does the food stay hot?

Challenge yourself!

Work in pairs. Talk about how to finish each sentence starter above to retell the information.

The lunches are made by workers' families at home.

Street foods

Let's talk

Look at this Street Food Market menu. What would you like for lunch? Why?

STREET FOOD MARKET

Pizza	Burger	Taco	Sweet
• Chicken and peppers	• Vegetarian	• Chicken	• Ice cream
• Vegetarian	• Spicy chicken	• Fish	• Doughnut

  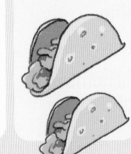  

 Would you like a doughnut, Guss?

No, thank you. I would like a vegetarian burger.

Hint

Vegetarian food means food with no meat. A **vegetarian** means a person who does not eat meat or fish. How does the beginning of the word help you to understand the word's meaning? What is the word for **vegetarian** in your language?

Practise

1 Write what you have for lunch at school.

2 Write what you have for lunch at home.

3 What street snacks do you like?

27

Use of English

Quantifiers: *a few*, *few*, *a little*, *little*

Learn

We use **quantifiers** when we want to tell someone about the **number** or **amount** of something.

We can use these words to mean a small number or amount of something.

a few | few | a little | little

Countable plural nouns	Meaning	Uncountable nouns	Meaning
few	not many/not enough	little	not much/not enough
A few	a small number/ enough	A little	a small amount/ enough

There are **few** snack choices today.

We have **little** money.

There are **a few** tasty ones over there.

I will share **a little** of my water.

Practise

Complete the sentences using the correct quantifier. Write them in your notebook.

1 Only _____ of us have hot lunch at school.
2 _____ people eat meat for lunch.
3 I like _____ water with my food.
4 We have _____ time to eat our lunch!
5 Sometimes we eat _____ sweet treats too.

Jenang is popular in Indonesia.

Challenge yourself!

Write four sentences about street food. Each sentence should use one of the quantifiers meaning 'some'.

Inviting: *Would you like to ...?*

Learn

When we want to invite somebody to do something we ask:
Would you like to ...?

Inviting	Verb	The activity or event
Would you like to ...	have	a picnic?
	eat	a snack?
	make	a pancake?
	buy	a drink?

Practise

Write a list of questions that invite someone to do something. Use these verbs.

(have) (eat) (make)

(buy) (drink) (share)

Let's talk

Use your list and work with a partner to invite each other to do different things.

Would you like to share this orange?

Yes, please! I'd love to!

No, thank you. I'm not hungry!

Reading

A Roman banquet

Practise

Read about a Roman feast called a banquet.

Salve! I am Marcus and this house is where I live and work. I sleep in the kitchen – it is lovely and warm. Decimus, the cook, woke me early this morning by banging pots and pans about in the kitchen. We're having a big banquet tonight so there is lots to do.

I must set up the banquet room. We arrange the couches in a large U-shape around the table. There is one couch for the family and next to it is one for the most important guests. We put beautiful cushions on the couches so our guests will be comfortable.

My favourite part of the banquet is when Decimus brings in the roast swan on a huge platter … and sings at the same time!

After eight hours, the last course has been eaten and the guests are preparing to leave.

It's not bedtime for me yet. We still need to clear up the banquet. I help Decimus wash up all the pots and pans. He has a surprise for us – he saved some honey cakes from the banquet! It was a fun day, but tiring too. I will sleep well tonight. Goodnight!

Hint

Ancient Romans spoke Latin. They greeted each other by saying **Salve**! In Italy, people still say *Salve!* as a way of saying 'Hi!'

Decimus means 'tenth' in Latin.

Do you know?

At banquets, Ancient Romans would lie down on couches to eat and talk. Here are some dishes the guests would eat.

Hint

Dormice is plural for dormouse.

Menu

Starters
Cheese with figs

Dandelion salad

Stuffed dormice in a honey and poppyseed dip

 *

Main course
Roast swan

Green beans in mustard

Roast wild boar with pepper

Cabbage with leeks and coriander

 *

Dessert
Honey cakes

Peeled grapes

Custard pudding

Practise

Answer my questions.

1 What is my name?

2 Where do I sleep?

3 Why do I like it there?

4 What is happening tonight?

5 What does *Salve*! mean? How do you say this in your language?

6 What does **Decimus** mean? Why do you think cook is called this?

7 What is my favourite part of the banquet?

8 What is our surprise at the end of the banquet?

Challenge yourself!

Find out more about how the Romans lived. Look online and in books.

Writing

Plan and write a story

Do you remember?

We can use connectives to link parts of sentences and to tell the correct order of what happens.

(when) (before) (after) (then)

> We have so much to do **before** the guests arrive.

Practise

Work with a partner. Share your ideas about the order of the sentences and how you will finish each sentence. Use your own ideas.

Planning your writing	Sentence starters	How to finish each sentence
1 Introduction	*Salve!* I am _____ and this house is where I live and work. I …	
2 Setting up the banquet room.	Before the guests arrive, I must set up the banquet room. I …	
3 The menu	Then we plan the menu and cook. This is what the guests will be eating: …	
4 Tidying up	When the guests have gone, we …	
5 A surprise!	After we have tidied up, cook has a surprise for us. It is …	

Practise

1 Plan to write your own story like the one written by Marcus. Copy the chart and finish each sentence with your own ideas.

2 Write your story in your notebook. Use your chart to help you. Draw pictures for each part of your story.

Try this

Work in pairs.

1 Look at the banquet menu on page 31.

2 Choose one dish. Talk about how you think the Romans cooked it.

3 Write a recipe for the dish. Think about these things:

- Ingredients
- What you need
- What to do.

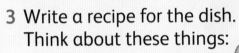

4 Make a poster of your recipe. Use pictures or drawings to show different parts of your recipe.

5 Present your recipe to the class.

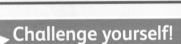

Challenge yourself!

1 Read your story again. Ask yourself these questions:

- Does my story make sense?
- Do the connectives link the sentences?
- Is my spelling correct?
- Is my handwriting neat?

2 What can you improve? Ask what a partner thinks too.

What can you do?

Read and review what you can do.

✔ I can talk about different sorts of feasts.

✔ I can offer things and invite people to do things.

✔ I can use countable and uncountable nouns and quantifiers.

✔ I can read and explore words in poems and stories.

Unit 3 Homes

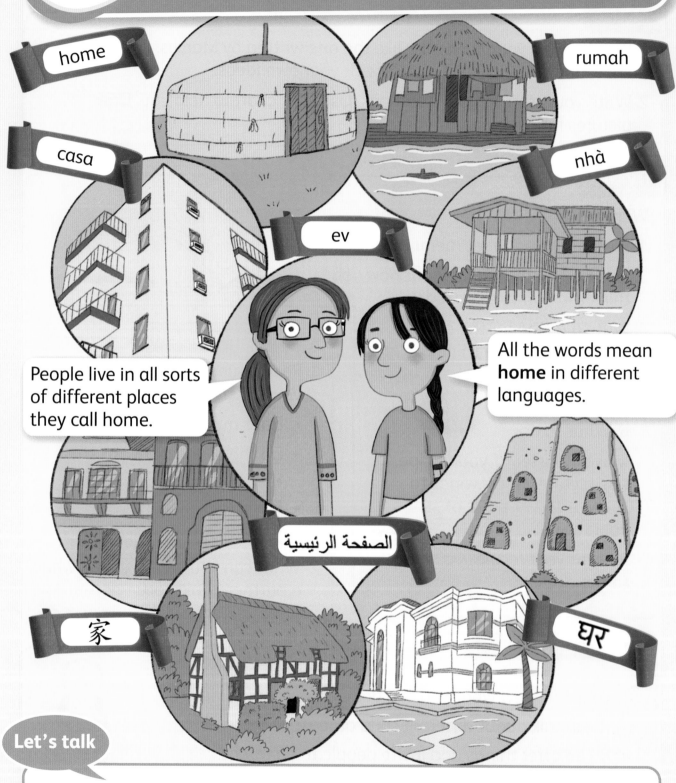

home

rumah

casa

nhà

ev

People live in all sorts of different places they call home.

All the words mean **home** in different languages.

الصفحة الرئيسية

家

घर

Let's talk

Talk about these different homes from around the world. Describe them. Where is your home? How do you say **home** in your language?

Listening and speaking

Different homes

People all over the world live in different kinds of homes.

 a round tent

floating homes made from reeds

home on stilts

 cave homes

a villa

stacked homes

 apartments

a cottage

Let's talk

Choose one home that you like. Talk about it with a partner.

I really like the apartments because we have homes like that in Santiago. They are modern. You have friends who live above you and friends who live below you. Friends everywhere!

We have an aunty who lives in an apartment like that.

Practise

Listen to this poem called *Living-places*. Make a list of all the living-places it mentions.

Challenge yourself!

1 Try to say or write one more thing about each picture.
2 Draw another type of home and write a caption for it.

Use of English

Imperatives

Do you remember?

We use an **instruction** when we are telling someone to do something.

Tell me who lives here.

We use a **command** when we strongly tell someone to do or not to do something.

Don't go up the stairs! **Stop!**

We use the **imperative** form of the verb for instructions and commands.

Practise

Sort the imperatives into the sets shown in the table.

stir · fold · hop

colour · relax · add

turn · pour · tear

skip · paint · bake

Imperatives when we are talking about ...		
cooking	making things	sport and exercise
mix	draw	run

Let's talk

Look at the pictures on page 37 and talk about them with a partner. Use these imperatives about speech to tell your partner what to do. Take turns.

Tell me ... · Describe ...

Point to ... · Explain ...

Say what you think about ....

Say what you think about the house in picture A.

Practise

1 Read these short texts about the homes in the pictures. Match each speaker to their home.

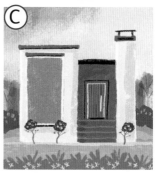

① Welcome to our home. Let's look around. Come with us.

Go through the grand front door. Climb the stairs.

Turn left for the living room and turn right for the dining room. Choose one of these rooms. Sit down and we will have tea.

② It's a good day! You can see my home behind me. It has a tin roof and a small door. Step inside and look around.

③ Good morning. This is my home. It is small and neat and it has everything I need. Look at its modern design. Come inside through the door round the back. There is one room with a window. Look out of the window. The room has a fire to keep me warm in the winter. Look at the little chimney.

2 Find the imperatives in each text.

⭐ Challenge yourself!

Imagine you live in a castle.

Write instructions for visitors so they know where they can go and where they must not go. Tell them what to see and do.

Listening and speaking

Making homes and buildings

Practise

Listen to the poem *This is my little house.*

1 Follow the instructions to make hand actions to go with the poem. Use these pictures to help you.

2 Practise saying the poem and making the hand actions until you are very good at doing both together.

Let's talk

Architects design buildings for us. Before they build a home, they make a small model. Talk with a partner about how these models are made.

1 What do you think they might be made from?

Hint

An **architect** is someone who designs homes.

2 What other things could you use to make model houses?

Practise

Work with a partner.

1 Talk about the parts of a house shown in the picture.

2 Say what you would do to build the house. Put your instructions in order. Use these words to help you.

(roof) (windows)

(door) (chimney)

(wall) (beams)

CUT & GLUE

HOUSE

1 cut out
2 glue

3 Write your instructions in your notebook. Follow them to build the house. Do the instructions work?

Try this

Make model houses using different materials. Make a class display.

Use of English

Prepositions of direction: *into, out of, from, towards*

We use some prepositions to talk about the direction things are moving in.

into	out of	from	towards
He looked **into** the window.	He looked **out of** the window.	He ran **from** the house.	He ran **towards** the house.

Do you remember?

Do you remember the traditional story of *Goldilocks and the Three Bears?*

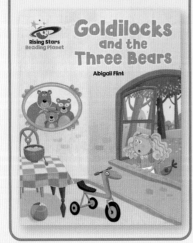

Practise

Complete the sentences about *Goldilocks and the Three Bears*. Choose from these prepositions.

into   in   out of   from   towards

1 Goldilocks was walking deeper and deeper _____ the woods when she saw a little cottage. She walked _____ the woods and _____ the cottage.
2 She looked through the door and went _____.
3 She looked around. She ate the porridge, she sat _____ the chairs and she tried the beds. She fell asleep and when she woke up, she saw three bears looking at her.
4 She ran _____ the house and never returned. The Bears were sad never to see her again.

Question tags

Learn

To turn a statement into a question, we can:
- write the statement as a question
- use a **question tag** at the end of the statement.

We often use a question tag to double-check what we think we know is true.

Statement	Question	Statement with question tag
The bears **are** out.	**Are** the bears out?	The bears are out, **aren't they**?
You **know** that story.	Do you **know** that story?	You **know** that story, **don't you**?

If the statement is positive, the question tag is negative.

Question tags:	Simple present *be*	Simple present other verbs
I	..., aren't I?	..., don't I?
You	..., aren't you?	..., don't you?
He/She/It	..., isn't he/she/it?	..., doesn't he/she/it?
We	..., aren't we?	..., don't we?
You	..., aren't you?	..., don't you?
They	..., aren't they?	..., don't they?

Practise

Say and write the question tags for these sentences. Use the verbs in the table above.

1 The house is empty.

2 Goldilocks eats the porridge.

3 This chair is too big.

4 We know how the story ends.

5 The bears chase Goldilocks out of the house.

6 Goldilocks feels scared.

Reading

Read about an adventure

Let's talk

Work with a partner. Look at the pictures and talk about them. They are about a girl who has an adventure. The pictures are not in the correct order.

Practise

Listen to and read the story.

① Anna sat on the doorstep of her house. She was very bored. She lived in a beautiful home, but there was nothing to do.

② She went up to her bedroom and lay on her bed. Out of the corner of her eye, she saw something blue on the floor. There was a book too. Anna jumped up to take a closer look.

③ She picked up the blue pencil and started drawing. She imagined that she could draw a way out of her bedroom … She drew a door in the book. The drawing became a real door. She opened it.

④ On the other side of the door there was a road! Anna stood for a minute with the blue pencil in her hand. The road had trees and lights. She saw a bridge on a lake and ran towards it.

⑤ When she got there, she discovered a locked gate with no key. 'Well, I can always draw a key with my blue pencil, can't I?' she said to herself. And she did. She opened the gate. In the distance she saw a magnificent royal palace on an island.

⑥ The palace was too far to walk. 'I can draw a bicycle,' she said. And she did. She hopped on and rode away. When Anna arrived at the palace, the guards at the entrance shouted, 'STOP!' What should she do next?

Practise

Answer these questions.

1 Where was Anna sitting?
2 What did she see in her bedroom and what did she do with it?
3 What did she want to draw her way out of?
4 What was on the other side of the door?
5 What did she have to draw next?
6 What sort of place did she arrive at?
7 What did the guards command her to do?

Try this

Split the class into two groups.
1 Group 1 reads the story aloud together. Group 2 acts out what Anna is doing.
2 Then swap.

Challenge yourself!

1 Reread the story.
2 Match each box of text to a picture.

Writing

Write about an adventure

Look at more pictures from *Anna's adventure*. Write a caption for each picture.

①

②

I think the king asks Anna to help find his stolen crown.

Practise

1 Talk with your partner and agree on answers to these questions.

- Who does Anna meet at the royal palace?

- What is the problem?

- What does Anna draw to help solve the problem?

- What happens at the end?

2 Now write your story ending in your notebook. Use the answers to the questions to help you.

3 Draw pictures and write a sentence or two for each picture. Make it an exciting end to your story!

Challenge yourself!

Write a sentence or two about what you would draw if you had a blue pencil like Anna's. Say why.

Do you know?

There are storybooks that tell a story in pictures and with a few or no words. This means you can tell the story in different ways and in different languages.

What can you do?

Read and review what you can do.

✔ I can talk about homes and buildings.

✔ I can use commands and instructions.

✔ I can use prepositions of direction and tag questions.

✔ I can read a story and write a new ending.

Review 1

Practise

Read and complete the sentences.

(out of) (Would) (apartment) (to eat) (to go) (window)

(from) (made) (swimming)

1 Banko and Jin like _____ to the beach. They enjoy _____ in the sea.

2 Jin always tells Banko, 'Don't swim too far _____ the beach.'

3 Last Saturday, Guss and Elok _____ pancakes. Elok loves _____ coconut pancakes!

4 Guss asks Elok, '_____ you like a few strawberries too?'

5 Sanchia and Pia's aunty lives in an _____ on the 10th floor. Sanchia likes to look _____ the window.

6 Pia's aunty reminds Pia, 'Be careful! Don't fall out the _____!'

Try this

Look at the picture and answer the questions.

1 What did they do last weekend?

2 What did they eat and drink?

3 How much orange juice is there?

4 How many bananas are there?

5 Would you like to share their picnic? Why?

6 What do you want to tell them to do? Write an instruction.

Practise

Match the questions and answers.

1 Would you like to share a dosa?
2 He is on holiday, isn't he?
3 Would you like some ice cream?
4 Would you like a little water?
5 Would you like to visit Indonesia?
6 You know that girl, don't you?

a Yes, I do. She lives in the apartment below.
b Yes! We can visit Elok and Guss.
c No, thank you. I'm not hungry.
d Yes, he is! He's in Chile.
e Yes, please. I'm thirsty.
f No, I don't like cold food.

Let's talk

Read the questions and discuss with a friend.

1 What do you enjoy doing?
2 Where did you go on your last holiday?
3 What did you do before school yesterday?
4 What did you do after school yesterday?
5 Describe your home.
6 What's your favourite food. Why?

Challenge yourself!

How many countries in the world do you know? Point and say the names of the countries you know.

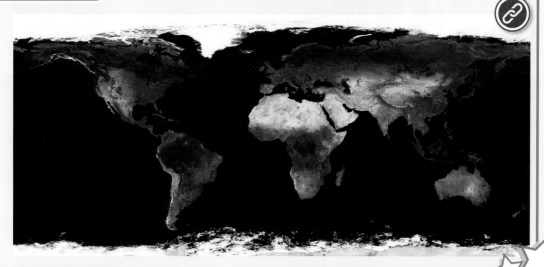

The moon is a ball of rock that goes round and round the Earth.

The sun is a flaming ball of gas. We are learning to use its energy!

Let's talk

Talk about the sun and the moon. When in the day do you see each one? Which is bigger – the sun or the moon? Why are they important?

Listening and speaking

Exploring the sun and the moon

Learn

We live on the Earth, which is one of many objects in space.

(solar system) (star) (planet) (moon)

Practise

Listen to Banko and Jin talking about the sun and the moon. Look at the facts below. Which ones are about the sun? Which ones are about the moon?

(closest star to Earth)

(a ball of rock)

(goes round the Earth)

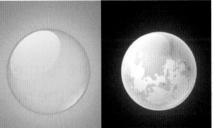

(a dry, dusty place)

(only star in the solar system)

(never look directly at it because it hurts your eyes)

Practise

Listen to Banko and Jin again. Find out what they want to know about the sun and the moon.

1 What's inside the sun?

2 How hot is it in the middle?

3 How do we take photos of the sun from space?

4 Why does the moon look as if it changes shape?

5 Are there other moons in the solar system?

6 What do space explorers do on the moon?

Let's talk

Work with a partner and talk about what you know about the sun and the moon.

Challenge yourself!

Look at the list of questions about the sun and the moon. Can you answer them? Find out the answers and write them in your notebook.

Use of English

Present continuous tense for the future

We can use the **present continuous tense** to talk about what people are doing. We can also use the same verb form (verb **be** + **–ing**) to talk about plans that we have made to do something in the future.

I'm staying up late this evening to see the full moon.

I'm inviting some friends here to watch it with us.

Which sentence is correct to talk about the future?

1 a Scientists are building space hotels on the moon next year.
  b Scientists build space hotels on the moon next year.
2 a We look for the full moon tonight.
  b We're looking for the full moon tonight.
3 a Are you joining us this evening?
  b Do you join us this evening?

Copy and complete each sentence in your notebook.

(are) (is) (are you) (you) (visiting) (am)

1 I _____ looking for stars tonight.
2 Banko _____ making his star model after dinner.
3 Are _____ star-gazing with us this week?
4 Jin and Banko _____ watching the Space Show on Friday, aren't they?
5 We are _____ the science museum next week.
6 What space badge _____ getting for your birthday?

Verbs with infinitive

Do you remember?

We often use the **infinitive** to talk about what something is for.

I use my sketchbook and pencil **to draw** the moon and stars.

Practise

1 Read these captions about space equipment.

We use a space probe to take photos of the sun.

We use a telescope to look at the night sky.

2 Point to the infinitive verb forms in the captions.

3 Write your own caption for this picture in your notebook.

Space explorers use a lunar module to land on the moon.

Challenge yourself!

1 Sort the words into the correct order to make two sentences for this picture.

can be make Stars joined up to patterns. a lion. pattern This is like

2 Do you know any other star pattern?

Listening and speaking

True space adventures

Listen to the space explorers talking. Point to each space explorer as you hear them speak.

Yuri Gagarin   Laika   Susan Helms   Neil Armstrong   Katherine Johnson

Listen again to the space explorers. Copy this table into your notebook, adding another line for each space explorer. Complete the table.

Name	Country	Date	What they did
1 Yuri Gagarin	Russia	1961	first man in space

Do more research on the five space explorers and add the information you find to your table.

Let's talk

Work with a partner.

1 Listen to information about the International Space Station (ISS).

Solar panels to make electricity

Built from different parts joined together

Laboratories for science experiments

2 Talk about the ISS:

a Which country built the ISS?

b What is inside the ISS?

c For how long do space explorers stay on the ISS?

d Can we see the ISS from Earth?

Hint

The word **orbit** means **to go round**.

Do you know?

The ISS:

- takes 90 minutes to orbit the Earth
- travels at a speed of 27 500 km an hour
- has an orbit height of 408 km above the Earth.

Try this

Work in small groups. Make a model space station out of anything you can find. What will you use to make each part?

Challenge yourself!

Find out more about the ISS. Make a poster to share what you find out.

Use of English

Have to and *don't have to*

Do you remember?

An obligation is when we must do something. It is the rule.

We use **have to** when we **must** do something.

We use **don't have to** when we **don't need to** do something.

Space explorers **have to** wear spacesuits in space.

Space explorers **don't have to** travel alone.

Practise

Rewrite these sentences about space explorers in your notebook, adding **have to**.

Space explorers learn to operate the technology on the ISS. They learn how to cope in a medical emergency. They also need to learn Russian, because they travel to and from the ISS in Russian rockets.

Let's talk

Talk about things people **have to** do to become space explorers. Say what they **don't have to** do too.

study science

sleep in sleeping bags strapped to the wall

get fit and healthy

get used to floating around

train for years

learn to fly a plane

Adjectives for comparing

Do you remember?

We use comparatives when we want to compare things.

The sun is a million times **bigger** than the Earth.

We use superlatives when we want to say which thing is top in a group.

The sun is the **closest** star to the Earth.

Words ...	of one syllable	of two syllables ending in y	of two syllables or more
What you do	Add **er** and **est**	Drop the **y** and add **ier** and **iest**	Use more and the most
Example	bright brighter brightest	shiny shinier shiniest	interesting more interesting the most interesting

Be careful – some words are irregular!

many or much/more/the most	good/better/the best

Practise

Sometimes the moon passes between the sun and the Earth. It blocks out the sun's light and the sky gets darker. This is a solar eclipse.

1 Talk about the picture using comparatives and superlatives. Use these words.

dark	light	round	thin	little	many
darker	lighter	rounder	thinner	less	more
darkest	lightest	roundest	thinnest	least	most

2 Which is brighter: picture 2 or 4? Which picture has the least light?

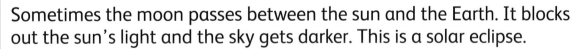

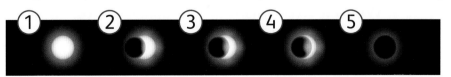

Reading

Why the sun and the moon live in the sky

Practise

Read the story as a class. Split the class into four groups.

Group 1 reads the part of the Narrator. Group 2 reads the part of Sun. Group 3 reads the part of Moon. Group 4 reads the part of Water.

Speaker	What you say
Narrator:	Many years ago, Sun and Water were great friends, and they both lived on the Earth together. Sun often used to visit Water, but Water never returned the visits.
Sun:	Why do you never visit me?
Water:	If you want me to visit you, you will have to build a **bigger** house. But I warn you that it will have to be the **biggest** house on the Earth. I have lots of family and friends and we take up a lot of room.
Narrator:	Sun promised to build the biggest house on the Earth and went to tell his wife, Moon.
Sun:	I have promised to build the **biggest** house on the Earth so that our friend Water and all his family and friends can visit us.
Moon:	It is the **best** surprise ever! We will be happy to welcome Water and his family and friends. Let's start building the **biggest** house on the Earth.
Narrator:	When it was finished, Sun asked Water to visit them.
Water:	I am here, Sun! Is it safe for me and my family and friends to flow into your house?

Practise (continued)

Sun and Moon:	Yes, you may all come in!
Narrator:	The water began to flow in, followed by the fish and all the other water animals. Very soon, the water was knee-deep in the house.
Water:	Is it **still** safe for us to keep flowing into your house?
Sun and Moon:	Yes please come into our house! You are most welcome.
Narrator:	So Water and all his family continued to flow in. When the water was at the level of a man's head, Water spoke again.
Water:	Is it **STILL** safe for us to keep flowing into your house?
Sun and Moon:	Yes, the more the merrier!
Narrator:	So more and more of Water's friends came in, until Sun and Moon had to sit on top of the roof of their house. When the water flowed over the top of the roof, Sun and Moon were forced to go up into the sky. And that is why the sun and the moon live in the sky.

Let's talk

There are lots of stories about the sun and moon in different countries around the world. Some people say this story is an old Chinese story. Other people say it is an African story. Do you know this story or one like it? Tell it to your partner.

Try this

Now act out the story. You need five groups:

- Narrator
- Sun
- Moon
- Water
- Water's friends and family.

Do you need any props?

Writing

A story about the sun and the moon

Practise

Work with a partner.

1 Look at the pictures.

2 Take turns to retell the story of why the sun and the moon live in the sky.

3 Write a sentence for each picture to retell the story.

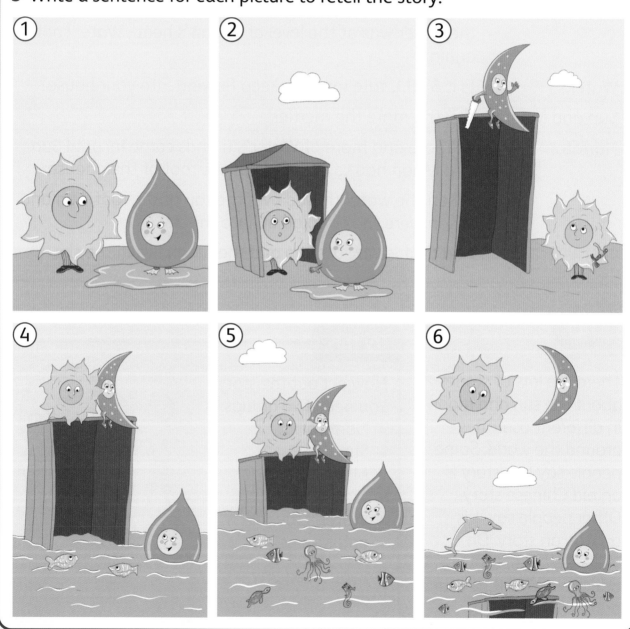

Challenge yourself!

1 Write these sentences in your notebook.

2 Listen and fill in the missing words in the sentences. Each missing word is one we use a lot in English. Remember to check your spelling.

_____ years ago, Sun and Water _____ great friends, and _____ both lived on _____ Earth together.

If you _____ me to visit _____, you will _____ to build a bigger house.

Try this

Listen to the instructions about how to spin like the Earth in a day. Work as class to do this until everyone understands how it feels to be the spinning Earth.

What can you do?

Read and review what you can do.

✓ I can talk about the sun, the moon and space.

✓ I can use the present continuous to talk about the future.

✓ I can read and act out a play in a group.

✓ I can write sentences to retell a story.

In Indonesia, we learn gamelan.

I play the traditional drums.

Let's talk

Which musical instruments do you play? Which musical instrument would you like to learn to play? Which is your favourite musical instrument? Say why.

Listening and speaking

Exploring instruments

Learn

Different bands may use different musical instruments.

brass band 1 string quartet 2 gamelan 3 gong 4

bonang 5 gangsas 6 kendang 7

rebab 8 celempung 9 jazz band 10 folk band 11

Practise

Listen to Guss and Elok talking about music at school. Then answer the questions.

1 What does Elok's teacher do to make music fun?

2 Does Guss like practising alone or in a group?

3 Which instrument do they each want to learn?

4 What does Guss want to be?

Let's talk

Work in pairs.

Choose an instrument from page 60. Describe it to a partner, but do not say its name. Can they guess which instrument you have chosen?

It's round and shiny. It's made of metal. You bang it with a kind of stick. What is it?

Try this

1 Listen to and sing the song *The music players.*

I am the music boy. I come from down your way. And I play …

What do you play?

I play the piano. Pia–pia–piano– piano–piano! Pia–pia–piano– pia–piano!

2 Then sing verses for other instruments. Make up the way you split the word so that it fits the rhythm!

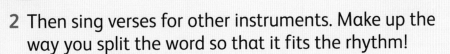

gamelan saxophone tambourine

Use of English

Present simple tense

Do you remember?

We use the **present simple tense** to talk about:

- **routines**, which are things we do at the same time
- **habits**, which are things we often or always do
- **states**, which are our opinions, our senses or how we feel.

> I **love** my new earphones.

> I **sing** in the choir.

> I **have** piano lessons on Wednesdays.

For the third person – he, she or it:

- add **–s**, **–es** or **–ies** to the verb
- add **–es** if the verb ends in **s**, **ss**, **sh**, **ch**, **x** and **o**
- add **–ies** if the verb ends in **y** after a consonant.

> He play**s** it well.

> He teach**es** us to play.

> He carr**ies** his saxophone.

Practise

1 Sort the sentences into the correct list.
   a I play the saxophone every day.
   b I play in a band.
   c I try very hard.
   d It sounds amazing.
   e She plays the drums.
   f She loves music.
   g She practises with us every week.

2 Copy the table and the sorted sentences into your notebook.

Routines	Habits	States
I have trumpet lessons on Mondays.	I listen to music.	I love the sound of gamelan.

3 Write your own sentences in the last three rows.

Practise

Write each sentence in your notebook. Fill in the missing word.

plays   is   writes

loves   names

1 Ed Sheeran _____ an English singer and songwriter.

2 He _____ his own songs.

3 He _____ the guitar.

4 He _____ all his guitars.

5 He _____ playing with LEGO bricks.

Try this

Change these sentences into the third person: **he** or **she**. Add the correct ending to the verb.

She studies music.

1 We study music.

2 We try to form a band.

3 We find the players.

4 We search for a hall to practise in.

5 We practise on Wednesdays.

6 We are superstars on Saturdays.

7 We love the songs we write and play.

Gerunds

Do you remember?

When we want to say what we **like doing** or what we **don't like doing**, we use the verbs **like**, **love**, **prefer** or **don't like** + **–ing**.

Pronoun	Verb	Gerund
I You	don't like like love prefer	
He She It	doesn't like likes prefers loves	**verb** + **ing** playing the trumpet.
We You They	don't like like love prefer	

Let's talk

Work with a partner and look at these musical instruments. Talk about what you like, love or prefer playing.

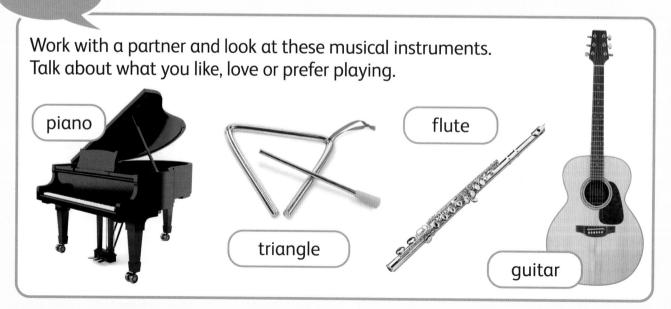

piano

triangle

flute

guitar

Practise

1 Read these captions about this pop star.

Super Sita loves performing.

Super Sita enjoys dressing up for a show.

Super Sita loves writing her own songs.

Super Sita enjoys playing the piano.

2 Match the captions to the pictures and copy them into your notebook.

①

②

③

④

Challenge yourself!

Write about your favourite pop star in your notebook. If you don't have one, then make one up! Use the present tense and gerunds.

Listening and speaking

Musical choices

Practise

1 Listen to the children talking about what music they enjoy listening to.
2 Match the characters to their opinions.

 Teacher   Farah   Elok   Adika   Cindy   Budi

① I like playing the trumpet.

② I only like modern music.

③ I love old-fashioned folk music.

④ I prefer rock music.

⑤ I love dance music.

⑥ In my opinion, classical music is boring.

Practise

1 Copy this table into your notebook.
2 Listen to the music. Fill in the table for each piece. Share your opinions with the class.

 I love dance music because I like dancing.

Track	Marks out of 10	I love it because …	I don't like it because …
1 Trumpet music			
2 Folk music			
3 Dance music			
4 Classical music			

Practise

1 Read about this famous singer.

Eunice Waymon was born in North Carolina, USA in 1933.

She started to play the piano when she was just three years old. She wanted to be a classical pianist and applied to a famous music school, but she was turned down. Eunice strongly believed that it was because she was a black person. She was angry and decided to start playing the piano and singing in clubs so people could hear her voice. She also changed her name to Nina Simone for when she was singing on stage. She became famous for performing songs with a message. The message was about the importance of treating everybody fairly. Her music was very popular. She died in 2003.

2 Talk about the text.

  a Where was Eunice born?

  b How old was she when she started playing the piano?

  c Why was she angry?

  d What were her songs about?

  e Why was that an important message?

Let's talk

Search online for Nina Simone songs. Listen to the music, the words and her voice.

Talk with a partner and ask these questions.

1 What do you think of her music?

2 What is your favourite song?

3 Do you have a favourite line? What is it?

Challenge yourself!

1 Search online for the words of a song you like. If you do not know one, try one of these songs:

> *Let it go* by Idina Menzel

> *Happy* by Pharrell Williams

2 Try to write some of the sentences you hear and like.

Use of English

Defining relative clauses

When we want to add information about people, places and things in the same sentence, we begin with these words:

(which) (that) (where) (who)

- We use **which** for things.
- We use **where** for places.
- We use **who** for people.
- We can use **that** for things or people.

> Elvis Presley is a singer **who** is called 'King of Rock and Roll'.
>
> This is the guitar **which/that** Elvis first played.
>
> Mississippi is the state **where** Elvis grew up.

A defining relative clause is essential in a sentence to tell us who or what is being described. You can't leave it out!

Practise

Work with a partner.

1 Take turns to talk about these tables. Match the correct parts to make sentences about these famous music makers.

2 Write the sentences in your notebook.

Sentence beginning	Which word?	Which end to the sentence?
Elvis is the music maker	**where**	was in the music charts for seven months.
All Shook up is the track	**which/that** **who/that**	you can visit the Elvis museum.
'Graceland' is		influenced other music makers.

Practise (continued)

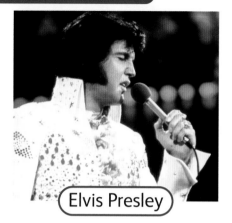

Elvis Presley

Elvis Museum, Graceland

Bob Dylan

Paintings by Bob Dylan

Sentence beginning	Which word?	Which end to the sentence?
Bob Dylan was the songwriter	where which /that who/that	he became famous for.
There is an art gallery in London		wrote a song for the singer called Adele.
Like a rolling stone is the song		you can see his paintings.

Challenge yourself!

1 Choose a famous music maker you like. Find out three things about them. If you don't have a favourite, then just pretend.

2 Write three sentences about the person using **where**, **which**, **who** and **that**.

Adverbs for comparing

Learn

When we compare two or more things, we use **comparative adverbs**.
We often use **more + –ly**. I think you are singing **more loudly** now.

We often use **than** to make the comparison clearer.

I think you sing **more loudly than** me.

When we want to say which is top in a group of three or more things, we use **superlative adverbs**.

We often use **the + –est**. Yes! I sing **the loudest** in my class.

Word	Adverb	Comparative	Superlative
loud	loud**ly**	more loudly less loudly	the loudest the least loudest
beautiful	beautifully	more beautifully less beautifully	the most beautifully the least beautifully

Be careful! Some words are irregular.

Word	Adverb	Comparative	Superlative
fast hard high	fast hard high	faster harder higher	the fastest the hardest the highest
good	well	better than	the best
bad	badly	worse than	the worst

Practise

Read about the children's band and write the correct words in your notebook.

The girl sings more (beautifully/beautiful) than the boys. The boys sing more (quiet/quietly) than the girl. The boy plays the drums the most (actively/active). The band plays music the (loudly/loudest)!

Practise

Copy the sentences into your notebook. Use the correct superlative adverb to complete each sentence.

1 He dances _____.

2 They dance _____.

3 They perform _____.

4 She drums _____.

5 We sing _____.

(the loudest) (the best)

(the most beautifully)

(the most actively) (the fastest)

Let's talk

Talk with a partner about your performing skills. Use the pictures for ideas.

She sings beautifully.

You perform the best in our class.

Challenge yourself!

What's your opinion?
In your class:

• who sings the most beautifully?

• who plays the piano the best?

• who dances the most skilfully?

Reading

A music festival for the whole family

Practise

Read about this music festival.

I'm so excited about the music festival this weekend. It sounds amazing!

Bali MusicFest

TICKET ONLY

Sunday 26 May

12 noon – 7 p.m.

At the Cricket Ground

Family friendly and Kids' Zone

Bands include:
Rock around the clock
Happy Girlz
Star Boys
Jaz
Jola

Let's talk

Talk about the music festival poster with a partner.

1 Would you want to go to this music festival with your family and friends? Why?

2 What else would you like to see at this music festival?

3 What makes the Bali MusicFest family-friendly and more fun?

Practise

Read a review. It tells us what Guss thought about the festival.

I thought the Bali MusicFest was awesome!

A review by Guss

Title of event: Bali MusicFest   **Date of event:** 26 May

Bands and acts
I thought there was a good line-up of bands and acts. The main stage was very busy and I couldn't always see the bands, but I could hear them! Some people sat on each other's shoulders. In my opinion, the best band was Star Boys and the worst performance was by Jaz.

Other things happening
There were lots of things happening to make it fun for the whole family. Elok liked the bouncy castle and little children were enjoying that too! I liked the magicians' corner.
There was a food and drink area and lots of toilets too.

Go or Miss?
Would I recommend this festival or would I say give it a miss?

I'd recommend this festival if you are looking for a good family day out. We had fun and there was something for everyone. I think Mum and Dad enjoyed it too, but they do like different music to us. I would prefer to see more bands next time.

Top tips: Buy your tickets before you go and get there early on the day to get close to the stage to see the bands.

Bali MusicFest   Sunday 26 May
12 noon – 7 p.m.
At the Cricket Ground
TICKET ONLY
Family friendly and kids zone
Bands include:
Rock around the clock
Happy Girlz
Star Boys
Jaz
Jola

Challenge yourself!

1 Read the review again and find these words and phrases.

a good line up   I'd recommend   give it a miss

2 What do you think they mean? How can you work out the meanings?

Writing

A poster and a review

Practise

Work in groups.

1 Look at the posters. Which event would you choose to go to? Why?
2 Do the posters give you all the information you need?
3 Write a list of the information that is missing from the posters.

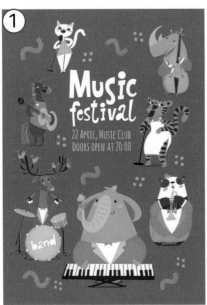

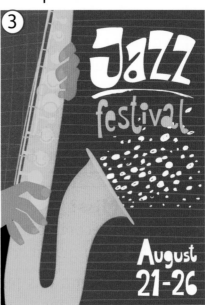

Practise

Work with a partner. Create a template for a poster. Make sure you include all the information that visitors will need.

(title)   (date)   (time)

(ticket price)   (where it is)

(events or acts)

Practise

Use your poster template to write your poster.

• Think about the pictures you want to use.
• Think about the style, shape and size of the letters.
• Have you included all the important information needed on your poster?

Try this

Use these headings to write a review of a festival that you have seen. If you haven't been to anything like this, then just pretend!

A review by _____

Title of event: _____   **Date of event:** _____

Bands and acts

Other things happening

Go or Miss?

Top tips

What can you do?

Read and review what you can do.

✔ I can talk about music and music makers.

✔ I can use adverbs to compare things.

✔ I can use **who**, **which**, **that** and **where** to add information to a sentence.

✔ I can read and write posters and reviews.

Let's talk

Talk about stories from the past. What stories like this do you know? Do you like stories about people or animals best? What is your favourite story?

Listening and speaking

What's the book about?

Practise

Listen to the woman who works at the library. She is the librarian.

Point to each book on page 76 as she talks about it.

Practise

1 Choose three books on page 76. Draw them and write a caption to say what each one is about.
2 Talk about your captions with a partner.

This book is a legend from Africa. It is about a hunter.

Let's talk

Work in pairs.

1 Choose a book on page 76 or from your classroom library.
2 Describe it to a partner, but do not say its title. Can they guess which book you have chosen?

It's a story about Kings and Queens. Which book am I choosing?

Try this

1 Find a book in your school, class library or online, about a legend.
2 Make a bookmark. Write a sentence on the bookmark to say what the book is about.
3 Talk about your bookmark in a class discussion.

Book title: _____

_____

This book is about _____

_____

_____

_____.

My rating:

☆ ☆ ☆ ☆ ☆

Name: _____

_____

Use of English

Subordinate clauses: *when, before, after*

Learn

A **subordinate clause** tells us more about the present or past.

Sentence	Subordinate clause	New sentence
I like to read stories.	**before** I go to bed.	I like to read stories **before** I go to bed.
I enjoy reading legends.	**when** they are about animals.	I enjoy reading legends **when** they are about animals.
I looked at the pictures.	**after** I read the story.	I looked at the pictures **after** I read the story.

Practise

1 Listen to and read the story of *Maui and the Big Fish.*
2 Find the subordinate clauses in the story. Write these sentences in your notebook.

Maui had four older brothers, but they would never let him go with them when they went fishing. He really wanted to go.

Maui secretly made the strongest fishing line and hook in the world. He hid in his brothers' fishing canoe when he heard them coming. Then he jumped out to surprise his brothers when they were far out at sea.

His brothers were angry, but Maui said special words to bring them luck. Then they started fishing and the brothers caught many big fish. Then it was Maui's turn. He caught a giant stingray after just a few minutes. The brothers cheered for Maui when they saw his super strength. Maui caught five more big fish and each fish turned into an island before they returned to land.

Legend tells us the fish became the six islands of the Pacific Ocean: Maui, Molokai, Kuaii, Hawaii, Oahu and Lanai.

Maui became known as a hero after this.

Past continuous tense

Learn

We can use the **past continuous tense** to talk about the past. We use it for something that happened before and after another action.

Pronoun	+ past tense of the verb *be*	+ *ing* form of the verb
I	was	floating.
You	were	watching.
He/She/It	was	learning.
We/You/They	were	making.

Maui **was hiding** in the fishing canoe as his brothers rowed it out to sea.

Let's talk

Work with a partner. Take turns to be Maui and retell the story to each other.

I **was hiding** in the canoe when my brothers went fishing.

I **was waiting** to jump out and surprise my brothers.

I **was trying** to show my brothers how good I was at fishing.

I **was making** a fishing line in secret.

Challenge yourself!

Write the beginning of a story. Use the past continuous tense and a subordinate clause.

I was _____ when/before/after _____ .

Listening and speaking

The Great Hunter

Let's talk

1 Listen to this story about the *Great Hunter*.

2 Talk with a partner about the story. Describe the hunter. Describe what happens.

Practise

Work with a partner. Join these sentences using connectives. Write the complete sentences in your notebook.

1 The Great Hunter had not hunted for a few years	and its head was held high in the air.
2 Its skin was shiny	because someone shot our prince.
3 The arrow struck the impala	because his children had grown up and he and his wife now lived alone.
4 It circled the tree three times	but it did not fall.
5 We are sad	and then disappeared.

Let's talk

Sort these sentences into the correct order and retell the story.

1. The village people were sad.
2. The Great Hunter knew he had shot the prince.
3. He followed it to a baobab tree and it disappeared.
4. The Great Hunter lived in a village.
5. He never hunted again.
6. He went hunting and shot an impala.
7. An old man took the hunter to a village under the tree.
8. When the prince went to the forest, he changed into an impala.

Try this

Work in groups of six to act out the story of the *Great Hunter*.

People in the story

storyteller   impala   old man

villagers   Great Hunter

Places in the story

forest   baobab tree

village under the tree

Challenge yourself!

1 Find another story about an underground world.

2 Retell this story to a partner.

Use of English

Descriptions with *like*

I **liked** the story of the *Great Hunter*.

We can use **like as a verb** to talk about things we enjoy.

We can also use **look** + **like** to talk about how something looks.

The prince **looked like** an impala.

Practise

Do you know the stories about the mouse deer named Sang Kancil?

Sang Kancil is very clever and likes to play tricks on other animals. Tiger wants to eat him, but he always tricks Tiger. Sang Kancil tells Tiger that he is guarding special things for the King. Tiger believes him and gets very cross because Sang Kancil escapes each time. What does Sang Kancil tell Tiger each thing **looks like**?

Match each thing to what Sang Kancil says it looks like.

(snake)   (muddy puddle)   (wasps' nest)

①

② ③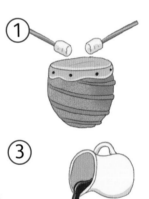

Try this

Draw an elephant. Write what the parts of an elephant look like.

I think an elephant's trunk **looks like** a snake.

(Its ear looks like a fan.)   (Its tail looks like …)   (Its legs look like …)

(Its body looks like …)   (Its trunk looks like …)   (Its tusks look like …)

Had to and *didn't have to*

Learn

Obligation is when we must do something. It is the rule.

We use **had to** when there was a strong obligation to do something in the past.

We use **didn't have to** when there was no obligation to do something in the past.

> Sang Kancil **had to** think quickly to trick Tiger.

> Tiger **didn't have to** believe Sang Kancil.

Practise

In another story, Sang Kancil tricks some crocodiles.

1 Read what he **had to** do.

> Sang Kancil was happy. He didn't have to worry about anything in the forest. He had to find a way to cross the river full of hungry crocodiles. Sang Kancil had to trick the crocodiles so that he could cross.

2 Write the sentences in your notebook. Underline the words **had to** and **didn't have to**.

Let's talk

Talk about Sang Kancil. Use these words to make sentences with **had to** and **didn't have to**.

- call friends to help him
- make Tiger believe him
- build a trap
- run away quickly
- think fast
- make normal things sound amazing

Reading

Running Rhino

Read this East African story, *Running Rhino* (African Animal Tales), by Mwenye Hadithi and illustrator Adrienne Kennaway.

1 Rhino was running on the Great African Plain. His eyes were not good so he ran at anything that moved. He was always chasing the other animals and they were getting cross.

2 One day, Rhino was running after something when Lion stopped him. 'You can't go on running about like this. You look so silly!' But Running Rhino said he had to run because it is what rhinos do. He didn't have to listen to Lion and he would challenge anyone to stop him. 'Then we will have a challenge!' roared the lion.

3 Lion asked the other animals who wanted to challenge Rhino. 'Who wants to stop Rhino running?' he asked. But the other animals all backed away when Lion said this. They were scared.

4 Then Tickbird spoke when she saw that the others were scared. 'I will challenge Running Rhino,' she said. 'If I win, he must go and live far away.' Rhino snorted, 'If I win, I will run as much as I like!' Tickbird challenged Running Rhino to a fight at sunrise and she went to find three friends to help her.

5 Tickbird was carrying three tiny gourds when she arrived for the challenge at sunrise.

6 Rhino stamped his feet and snorted. Tickbird tipped over one of the gourds and tipped out a mosquito. Rhino was still snorting when the mosquito bit him on the nose, but Rhino did not want to give up.

7 Tickbird tipped out the second gourd. A bee came out and stung Rhino on his tail. But Rhino did not want to give up.

Practise (continued)

8 Tickbird tipped out the last gourd. An ant came out and crawled up Rhino's leg and bit him behind his knee, under his tummy and on his horn.

9 Rhino was rolling on his back. He was itching and tickling. He gave up!

10 Tickbird flew onto Rhino's back when he was leaving. 'I will sit here and peck you when there is danger and you will know when to run and not run. I can help you not to run after everything. And so that is why tickbirds sit on rhinos' backs.

Practise

Work with a partner. Find these words in the story *Running Rhino*.
Match each word to its meaning.

1 gourd	**a** a kind of bird that sits on animals' backs
2 tickbird	**b** when your skin needs scratching
3 itching and tickling	**c** a big flat area of land
4 snorting	**d** a funny noise from nose
5 plain	**e** a fruit with a hard skin, like a pumpkin

Try this

Follow these instructions.

1 Imagine the story is going to be a film.

2 Use the ten parts of the story to create a film strip.

3 Draw ten boxes. In each box, draw a picture for each important part of the story.

4 Use the pictures to retell the story.

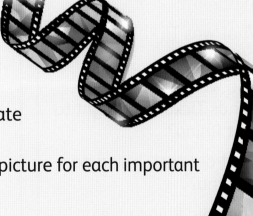

Writing

Writing about a story

Practise

1 Read the story of *Running Rhino* again.

2 Write the answers to these questions:

a Where was Rhino running?

b Why did Lion say Rhino had to stop?

c Why did the other animals not want to challenge Rhino?

d What was Tickbird's challenge?

e Who were the three friends Tickbird brought to fight Rhino?

f What did each friend do to Rhino?

g When did Rhino give up?

h Why did Tickbird go with Rhino?

Practise

1 Look at these pictures in a film strip.

2 Write a caption for each picture. Use these words and phrases to help you, but add your own too.

Names	Running Rhino Lion Tickbird
Places	Great African Plain Far away
Story beginning	One day … Long ago …
Story ending	And that is why … And that is the story …

Try this

1 Find these words and phrases in the story.

(look like)   (had to)   (when she saw that the others were scared)

(but Rhino did not want to give up)   (was rolling)   (didn't have to)

2 Write the sentences you find and draw a picture for each one.

⭐ **Challenge yourself!**

The word **rhino** is short for the word 'rhinoceros'. What are the short words for these animals? Write the words in your notebook and draw a picture of each animal.

(crocodile)   (hippopotamus)   (chimpanzee)

What can you do?

Read and review what you can do.

✔ I can read, write and talk about stories from long ago.

✔ I can use the **past continuous** to talk about things happening **before** or **after** other things.

✔ I can say what things **look like**.

✔ I can use **had** to and **didn't have** to.

Review 2

Practise

Read and complete the sentences.

(are playing)   (was reading)

(to look)   (more beautiful)

(more beautifully)   (before)

(playing)   (who)   (moon)

1 Banko and Jin like _____ at the moon _____ they go to bed.

2 Banko thinks the moon is _____ than the sun.

3 Guss and Elok _____ in a jazz band at a music festival this weekend.

4 Guss loves _____ the trumpet, but Elok plays the trumpet _____ than Guss.

5 Pia _____ a story when Sanchia came into her bedroom.

6 Pia said the story was about a girl _____ liked to travel and went to the _____.

Try this

Look at the picture and match the sentences.

(Mary)   (David)   (John)

1 David is the boy …

2 The music room is the place …

3 The children have to …

4 The children are practising …

5 Mary plays the flute better …

6 John was playing the violin when …

a for a music concert on Saturday.

b who is wearing blue shorts.

c Mary played the wrong note.

d than John plays the violin.

e where the children play their instruments.

f practise every day.

Practise

Order the sentences.

1 teacher / person / to learn / helps us / is the / English. / Our / who
2 where / place / School / is the / we / English. / study
3 have to / Students / their / teacher. / listen to
4 The sun / more / the moon. / than / brightly / shines
5 the / loudly / string quartet. / The / more / brass band / plays / than
6 interesting / most / is the / *Great Hunter* / The / tale from the past.

Let's talk

Read the questions and discuss them with a partner.

1 What are you doing after school?
2 What were you doing before school?
3 What do you have to do every day?
4 What did you have to do yesterday?
5 What do you love doing?
6 What don't you like doing?

Challenge yourself!

What's your favourite story? Talk for one minute about your favourite story, the main characters, why they are important, and what happens to them in the story.

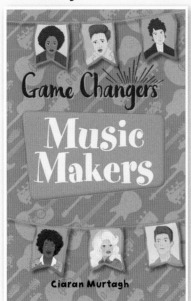

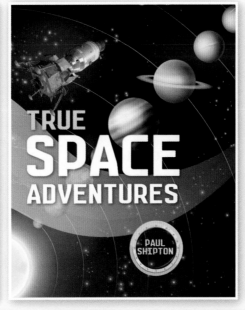

What can their robot do?

It can dance! But ours is better because it helps people.

Let's talk

Talk about the picture. What do you think Banko and Jin are doing? What do you already know about robots? What would you like to know about robots?

Listening and speaking

A robot workshop

Practise

1 Listen to the children talking about their robots.

2 Answer these questions.

  a Where is the competition?

  b How many teams are there?

  c What did the teams have to use?

  d How can Team Banjin's robot help people?

Try this

Can you walk like a robot?

Can you pick up something from the floor like a robot?

Can you dance like a robot?

Can you speak like a robot?

Let's talk

Work with a partner. Look at the robots on page 90. Then take turns to ask and answer these questions.

1 What do you think each robot can do?

Some robots are just toys.

2 Which robots look like they are just toys?

3 Which robots look like they can do a job for us?

4 What sort of robot would you like to build?

Challenge yourself!

Read the answers. Then ask a question for each one.

My question is: What can this robot do?

1 This robot can lift heavy things.

2 It's Team Banjin's robot.

3 This robot is the best.

4 Because building robots is fun.

Use of English

Be going to for plans

Do you remember?

We can use **will** to talk about plans we have as we are speaking.

What will we call our robot? I know! **We'll** call it Jinban.

Learn

We can use **be going to** when we talk about plans that we have already decided.

I know our robot is the best. I'm **going to** look at the other robots.

Are you **going to** build the robot's arms next?	Yes, I am. Yes, we are.	No, I'm not. No, we're not.

Let's talk

Pretend you are going to build a robot.

 Are you going to build a robot that lights up?

1 Are you going to build a robot that: — Yes, I am.
- talks?
- lights up?
- picks up things?
- walks?

2 Which things are you going to use? Use these words to help you.

 LED lights

springs

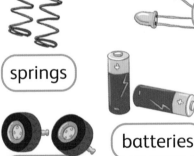 batteries — wires

 wheels

glue — cardboard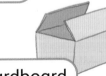

Practise

Write a list of the things you have chosen to use in a table like this.

1 Write what you are going to use each thing for. What else do you need?

2 Draw your robot. Add labels to show what each part is made of.

Recycled things	For my robot's …	Notes – other things I am going to need
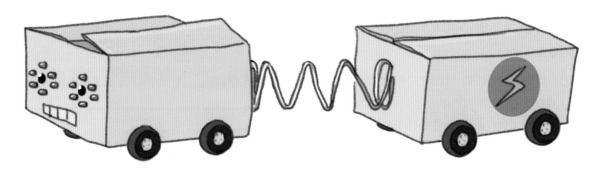 coloured wires	hair	Something to cut the wire

Challenge yourself!

1 Read about this boy who has a bionic arm.

Freddie Cook is eight years old and is the youngest person in the world to be fitted with a bionic arm.

Freddie is very excited about his new arm. He's going to do lots of new things with his friends and play like everyone else. He's going to 'high-five' everyone he meets.

Freddie is going to be a real tech hero with his 'Hero Arm'.

2 Write two questions you would like to ask Freddie using **going to**.

*

*See Acknowledgements page

Listening and speaking

World of Robots

Practise

Listen to and read this introduction. It is the starter for a set of books about a *World of Robots*.

Humans had to leave the planet fast. In the rush, a lot got left behind including Jango and his grandpa. Now they're stuck in a world that's almost completely flooded.

Robot ships roam the ocean. They gather anything they find, put it into crates and bring it to the docks. Jango, Izza and grandpa have to then sort it all out in their warehouse.

They find good things that can be used in the space stations. They recycle the rest. Every few weeks, a transporter comes to take the good things up to the space stations.

But sometimes things can go wrong …

Let's talk

Talk to a partner about the story introduction. What sorts of things could go wrong?

Challenge yourself!

Work with a partner. Match the words with their meanings.

Word	Meaning
1 introduction	pick up or collect
2 rush	the beginning
3 roam	where ships stay
4 gather	hurry
5 dock	where things are stored
6 crate	travel around
7 warehouse	a strong box

Let's talk

Work with a partner. Take turns to ask and answer questions about the story.

1 What are the characters' names?

2 Why do you think humans had to leave the planet fast?

3 What is the world like in the *World of Robots*?

4 What takes the good things up to the space station?

5 What do they do with the good things they find?

6 What do the robot ships do?

Challenge yourself!

Find more books about robots that you would like to read.

Let's talk

1 Listen to these book blurbs. A blurb tells you something about the story to make you want to read it.

2 Talk with a partner. Which book would you choose and why?

I would choose *Wild Robots*.

Why?

Mmmm … I'm not sure. Because I want to know about the wild beast!

Okay. That's a good answer!

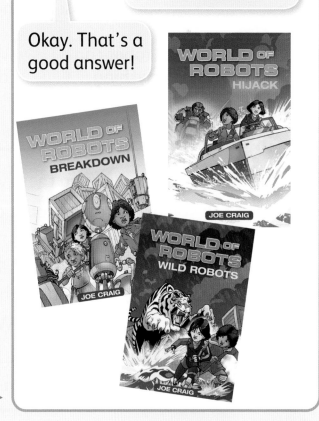

Use of English

Something, nothing, anything

Learn

We can use the words something, nothing or anything as pronouns or things.

Something	An unknown thing	Used in positive sentences	That team is building **something** special.
Anything	A thing of any kind	Used like 'something', but for more general things	You can build anything you like.
		Used in questions and negative sentences	Can I help with **anything**? I can't find **anything** wrong with it.
Nothing	Not one thing	Used at the beginning of a sentence as the subject	**Nothing** was happening.
		Used as the object	There is **nothing** to show.

 That robot can do **anything**.

Wow! There is **nothing** better to see!

Practise

Complete the sentences using these words. (something) (anything) (nothing)

1 What can you tell me about robot control?
_____, I'm not an expert.

2 I want to read _____ about robots.

3 Do you know _____ about the other teams?

4 There is _____ more to do. We have finished planning our robot.

5 It's too hard. I can't do _____.

6 I'll think of _____ brilliant in a minute.

Practise

1 Read about the World Robot Olympiad (WRO).

The World Robot Olympiad is a global competition. It first started in 2004 and now has more than 27 500 teams and over 100 000 young people involved each year. It is organised in over 75 countries.

Each season, there is a new theme and challenges. Themes can be anything, but this year it is SMART cities. You have to choose a challenge. You can choose to have your robot perform tasks, play football or help solve a real-life problem.

Teams from all over the world test their skills and make new friends at this exciting event. Teams can be two or three students and a coach.

The competition is nothing without you and your ideas! So sign up and get started.

Hint

global: worldwide

solve: give an answer

coach: teacher or a guide

2 Find the sentences that include the words: **something**, **nothing** or **anything**. Write them in your notebook.

Let's talk

Work in groups. Talk about the World Robot Olympiad.

1 Say three things you like about the WRO competition.

2 Say something you would change about the WRO.

3 Is there anything else you want to say about the WRO?

Reading

Robots in the news

Read this news report about an underwater robot.

FISH HELP TO POWER UNDERWATER ROBOTS

The US Navy has found a way to recharge underwater robots using fish waste, as well as other waste that lies at the bottom of the sea.

Underwater robots are helpful because they show us what underwater life is really like. They are usually powered by batteries but the power does not last very long. This means underwater missions have to be just a few weeks long.

The US Navy thinks it has solved this problem. It means that underwater robots can be sent on longer missions – up to eight months – to find out more about the bottom of the sea.

New batteries last for longer

As the waste breaks down, bacteria make an electric current. The electricity is sent to the tiny fuel cells and these make the power.

Meriah Arias-Thode, a scientist who works at the US Navy, called it 'a battery made from biology'.

Hint

recharge: add energy into a battery

battery: something that stores electricity to power other things

mission: a journey to do something special

bacteria: very small living things, often just one cell

Practise

Answer these questions in your notebook.

1 Who has found the new idea?
2 Why are underwater robots helpful?
3 What is the problem with underwater robots now?
4 What can the new underwater robots do?
5 Who said the new battery is, 'a battery made from biology'?

Try this

News report headlines need to grab our interest so we want to read the rest of report. Write a new headline for this story. Think about the letter style, letter size and colour.

THE POWER OF FISH WASTE

FISH WASTE POWER AND ROBOTS

Down at the bottom of the sea …

Let's talk

Work with a partner. Talk about how the news report looks.

1 What is the title or headline of this report?
2 What is different about the headline and the rest of the report?
3 What is the caption for the photograph?

Challenge yourself!

Find another news report that is about robots. Where can you look?

Writing

Writing a news report

Learn

Read this *Fact Box* about writing a news report.

Fact box

- Keep your headline short and interesting.
- Use the third person: he, she or it.
- Use the past tense.
- Split your report into small parts or paragraphs to help the reader.
- Use something someone has said.
- Use a photo with a caption.

Let's talk

1 Use the *Fact Box* as a checklist. Write the points in your notebook.

2 Read the report 'Fish help to power underwater robots' on page 98 again.

3 Find an example of each thing on your checklist.

4 Discuss with your partner. What did you notice?

The headline was interesting, so I wanted to read the report.

FISH HELP TO POWER UNDERWATER ROBOTS

Practise

1 Read this *Fact box* about another robot story.

Ai-Da

Headline	Robot artist gets first art exhibition
People	Name of robot: Ai-Da Artist: Aidan Meller
Place	Oxford, England
Fact 1	Ai-Da looks like a human. Her name links to two things: 1 AI or artificial intelligence (things that are built to be like humans) 2 Ada Lovelace, the first person to create a computer programme.
Fact 2	Ai-Da can draw what she sees. She can also create sculptures when linked to a 3D computer.
Fact 3	Ai-Da was built by a team of 15 people over two years.
What someone said	Aidan Meller: 'This work is as good as anything else we have seen from a robot.'

2 Write a news report about Ai-Da. Use the *Fact* box to help you.

3 Add extra information if you want to. Look at page 98 again to give you some layout ideas.

What can you do?

Read and review what you can do.

✔ I can read, write and talk about robots.

✔ I can use **be going to** for plans

✔ I can use **something**, **anything** and **nothing**.

✔ I can read and write newspaper reports.

Let's talk

What are Guss and Elok doing? Name the other activities. What do you know about outdoor adventures? Which adventure would you like to try?

Listening and speaking
Outdoor adventures

Practise

Listen to the children talking about their wild adventures.

Point to the activities on page 102.

- kayaking
- rock climbing
- zip-lining
- hiking
- orienteering
- mountain biking
- camping
- white-water rafting

Practise

Listen to this girl talking about her favourite kind of wild adventure. Write the ten missing words in your notebook.

> I like the idea of geocaching.

My favourite wild adventure hobby is geocaching. Do _____ know _____ that is?

It's a sort of high-tech treasure hunt. _____ follow numbers and letters on a map to look _____ clues to find the caches, which is the treasure.

We get the clues online _____ a special geocaching website. We use a GPS tracker or _____ phones to take _____ to the right place. Then we _____ to use our own skills to find the hidden treasure.

The treasure can _____ anywhere, _____ it is usually hidden in a wall or under stones in a box.

Challenge yourself!

1. What do you think the treasure might be?
2. What would you put in the box?
3. What sort of box would work best? Why?

> If you take something out of the treasure box, you should leave something too. What would you leave?

Use of English

Present perfect tense: *Have you ever ...?*

Do you remember?

We use the present perfect tense when we talk about something that started in the past and is still happening.

> I *have* **been** a climber for three years.

We often use it with **ever** to talk about our experiences.

> *Have* you <u>ever</u> **climbed** a mountain?

> No, **I've never climbed** a mountain.

Let's talk

Work with a partner. Look at the picture on page 102. Ask and answer questions about the activities. Begin with: **Have you ever ...?** Say yes or no.

> Have you ever kayaked?

> Yes, I have.

Practise

1 Copy this table into your notebook.
2 Listen to Elok.
3 Tick who has done each activity.

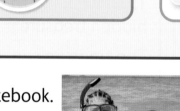

Have you ever ...	Elok	Amir	Ana
travelled in a hot air balloon?			
mountain biked down a volcano?			
found treasure when geocaching?			
kayaked down a river?			
snorkelled in the sea?			

Practise

Make your own chart like Elok's. Write four questions to ask three friends.

Try this

Play the game **Have you ever …?** in small groups.

1 Sit in a circle with one person holding a ball.
2 The person with the ball asks a question about a wild adventure.
3 Then they throw the ball to a classmate who answers with yes or no.

Have you ever hiked in a jungle?

Yes, I have.

⭐ Challenge yourself!

1 Read about this adventure.

I am Selah Schneiter. I am ten years old. I have climbed one of the toughest mountain climbs in the USA. It's called The Nose. I did it with my family in five days.

I hope my climb will inspire others to be active. Have you ever had a big goal like this? You just have to do it bit by bit.

2 Write two questions that you would like to ask Selah.
3 Write what 'big goal' you would like to achieve.

Listening and speaking

The man who went to sea with a hen

Practise

Listen to and read this story.
Have you ever heard a story like this before?

Five years ago, a French sailor decided to sail around the world. He bought an old boat and practised a little. Then he set sail alone.

Before he crossed the Atlantic Ocean, he stopped off in Spain. Some friends gave him Monique, a chicken. She would be a good friend and give him fresh eggs on his adventure.

The sailor and Monique became friends. He taught her to swim and surf. She gave him fresh eggs, which saved his life.

The sailor and Monique are planning their next adventure, but they haven't told the world what it will be yet!

Let's talk

Talk about these questions with a partner.
1 Do you think this story is true? Say why.
2 How can you find out if it is true or false?

I think this story is true/not true because …

Practise

Work with a partner. Take turns to ask and answer questions about the story.

1 What is the chicken's name?
2 Why did the sailor take a chicken with him?
3 What did they do together?
4 What or who would you take on a boat adventure?
5 Where did the sailor stop off?
6 How would you teach a chicken to swim?

Try this

Play the game **Listen and repeat**. Work with a partner.

1 Copy this table.
2 Cut up the table to make nine cards.
3 Colour three cards blue, three cards red, and three cards yellow. Keep the cards in colour sets.
4 Take turns to choose a card. One person reads the words and then the other person repeats the words from memory.

Hint

Check your pronunciation.

	Easy (colour blue)	Harder (colour red)	Hardest (colour yellow)
words	hen boat eggs	sailor adventure chicken	decided ocean world
phrase	five years ago	his adventure around the world	before he crossed the Atlantic Ocean
sentence	He bought an old boat.	The sailor and Monique became friends.	She gave him lots of eggs, which saved his life.

⭐ Challenge yourself!

Find more stories about wild and funny adventures.

Use of English

Adverbs to use with the present perfect tense:
never, yet, already, always

We can use the adverbs **never**, **yet**, **already** and **always** to talk about the time of any action: how often and when.

Adverb	Meaning	Example
never	Have not done it at any time	I have **never** sailed a boat.
already	Have done it before	I have **already** sailed a boat.
always	Have wanted to do it for a long time	I have **always** wanted to sail a boat.
yet	Haven't done it, but might do it one day	I haven't sailed a boat **yet**.

Have you ever seen a hen at sea?

No! I've **never** seen a hen at sea!

Let's talk

Talk about the pictures with a partner. Say four sentences for each picture using each of the adverbs above.

 1

 2

Practise

Copy and complete the sentences in your notebook. Use these words.

(never) (yet) (already) (always)

1 I have ____ seen an iceberg.
2 I have ____ wanted to learn to skate.
3 Have you visited another country ___?
4 Have you ____ learned to ride a bike?
5 I have ____ seen an eagle in the mountains.
6 We have ____ had an adventure holiday.

Practise

Write **true** or **false** for each sentence.

1 I've never wanted to win a gold medal.

2 I've always wanted to camp in the jungle.

3 I've ridden a camel, but I haven't ridden on an elephant yet.

4 I've already climbed a mountain.

5 I've always wanted to learn how to dive.

6 I've never wanted to swim with dolphins.

7 I've already learned how to mountain bike.

8 I've flown in a plane, but I haven't flown in a helicopter yet.

Try this

Learn this poem.

If you've ever met a crocodile
You'll know never to poke him.
To always be wary of his smile
And never, ever to stroke him.

Challenge yourself!

Complete each sentence.

1 I've never seen …

2 I haven't … yet.

3 I've always wanted to ….

4 I've already …

Reading

Fifty things to do before you are 11¾

Practise

1 Read this chart.

© National Trust Images

 I've already done a lot of these things!

Yes, me too. But I haven't set up a snail race yet!

Practise

Match the words to their meaning.

1 clamber   to block

2 spot   to look for

3 dam   to see

4 forage   to climb

Let's talk

Find the number on the chart for these adventures and talk about what you think they mean.

1 Go welly wandering.
2 Play pooh sticks.
3 Skim a stone.
4 Go on a scavenger hunt.
5 Find some funky fungi.

Hint

Use the badge picture on the chart to help you.

welly wandering

funky fungi

Practise

Use the chart on page 110. Write the answers in your notebook.

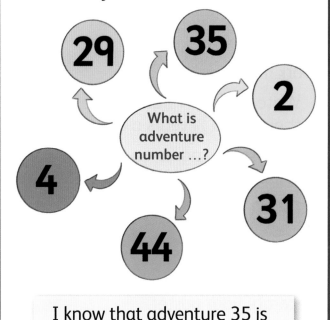

29 35
2
What is adventure number …?
4
44 31

I know that adventure 35 is 'Discover what is in a pond!'

Challenge yourself!

1 Find these words in the chart.

watch   roll   spot

2 Copy the sentence from the chart in your notebook.
3 Write a new sentence for the word's other meaning.

If we don't know the other meaning, we can look it up in a dictionary.

Writing

Writing an adventure chart

Let's talk

Work in groups.

1 Write a list of 15 adventures you think children should have had before they are 11¾ years old.

2 Discuss and agree on a picture for each adventure.

Practise

Work in groups.

Make a poster like this. Write and draw your ideas on the poster, and then decorate your poster.

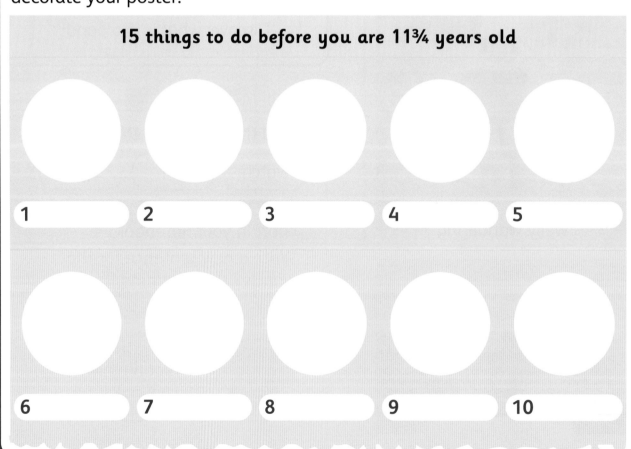

15 things to do before you are 11¾ years old

1   2   3   4   5

6   7   8   9   10

Practise

Check things you have done and things you want to do.

1 Use your chart from page 112 to check which things you have done.

2 Write a checklist with numbers 1–15 in your notebook.

Adventure	I have already done	Things I would like to do
1	✓	
2		

3 Tick the things that you have already done. Colour in the things that you still want to do.

4 How can you do the things you haven't done yet?

Challenge yourself!

1 Look back through this unit and choose your favourite adventure story.

2 Look back through this unit and choose the adventure that you would never want to try.

3 Write a paragraph explaining your choices.

4 Swap paragraphs with a partner. Give each other feedback.

What can you do?

Read and review what you can do.

✔ I can read, write and talk about wild adventures.

✔ I can use the **present perfect** to talk about time: **Have you ever** …?

✔ I can use **adverbs** to talk about time: **yet**, **never**, **already**, **always**.

✔ I can read and write an adventure poster.

Let's talk

Which school trips do Sanchia and Pia like best? Name the other trips. What do you already know about school trips? Which school trip would you choose?

Listening and speaking

Fun school trips

Practise

Listen to the children talking about their school trips.
Point to each picture on page 114 as they are speaking.

Practise

Look at page 114 again. Draw each sort of school trip and write
a caption for it. Use these words to help you.

(the zoo)   (a train ride)   (a boat trip)

(the theatre)   (a bus ride)   (the beach)

(a museum)

(a picnic in a park)

(a castle)   (a football stadium)

Let's talk

Choose one sort of trip that you like. Talk about it with a partner.

I really like visiting the theatre. I like it when we have to find our seats. We are very noisy and when it starts we have to be very quiet!

I like that too! I like it when the lights go down and the show is about to start.

Use of English

Future simple tense: *will*

Do you remember?

We use **will** to talk about the future. We can use it to do the following:

(predict) (mean the same as the word 'want') (make or talk about a promise)

 Do you think we **will** stay away for one or two nights?

 **Will** everyone be allowed to go?

 Yes, they **will!**

Practise

1 Read this letter from a school about a school trip.

Dear Class 4A

End-of-year school trip: Next Thursday

Please give this letter to your parents.
This year's end-of-school trip will be to an activity centre.
We will leave school at 8.30 a.m. and return at 4 p.m.
You won't need to bring food or bedding.
You will need to bring clothes for walking, boating, fishing and swimming.
Please arrive on time to get on the bus – we won't wait for latecomers!

We'll have a wonderful time!

Best wishes

Your Teacher

P.S. We will make sure that everyone keeps safe.

Hint

latecomers: people who are late
won't: the same as 'will not'

2 Find each use of the future simple tense in the teacher's letter. How many can you find?

Determiners: *each, every*

Learn

We can use the words each and every to talk about singular nouns. We use **each** to refer to individual things in a group or a list of two or more things. It is similar in meaning to **every**, but we use **every** to refer to a group or a list of three or more things.

Determiner	When	Example
each	When we talk about individual things or people in a group. The group is two or more people.	Group A has three students and **each** student will need to pack strong shoes.
every	When we talk about the whole group. The group is three or more people.	Group B has four students and **every** student will take turns carrying the bags.

In **every** group, there will be a leader.

Students will look after **each** other too.

Practise

1 Read about the activity centre.

ACTIVITY CENTRE

- The activity centre is set in beautiful countryside.
- You can see lakes and mountains everywhere.
- Every room has Wi-Fi and each one has a different view.
- The centre has two student blocks with about 50 students in each building.
- Every day is different and each student is offered an exciting mix of activities.

2 Find all the examples of **each** and **every**. Add a sentence of your own.

Listening and speaking

The Owl and the Pussy-cat trip

Practise

Listen to and read the beginning of this famous nonsense poem by Edward Lear.

The Owl and the Pussy-cat

The Owl and the Pussy-cat went to sea
In a beautiful pea-green boat,
They took some honey, and plenty of money,
Wrapped up in a five-pound note.

Try this

Learn the poem.
Split the class in two groups.
Group 1 says lines one and three.
Group 2 says lines two and four.
Say the poem out loud like this:

Group 1: The Owl and the Pussy-cat went to sea

Group 2: In a beautiful pea-green boat,

Group 1: They took some honey, and plenty of money,

Group 2: Wrapped up in a five-pound note.

Do you know?

Edward Lear was born in England and died in Italy. He was a painter and a poet. He had a pet cat, Foss.

Edward Lear (1812–1888)

118

Practise

Work with a partner. Answer the questions.

1 How did Owl and Pussy-cat travel?

2 What colour was the boat?

3 How could you describe the sea using two words joined together like pea-green?

4 What did they take with them?

5 What were the things wrapped up in?

6 Find two pairs of rhyming words in the poem.

Challenge yourself!

1 Listen to the poem again.

2 Draw what you hear.

3 Compare pictures with a partner.

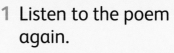
I imagined Owl to look like this!

I thought the boat would look like this.

Let's talk

Work with a partner. Say what you think.

① Where do you think Owl and Pussy-cat were going?

② What would you take on a sea journey like this?

③ They took honey and money. What else could they have taken?

④ What do you think about their planning?

Challenge yourself!

Find more poems by Edward Lear. Is there a poet you like from your country?

Use of English

Might, may, could for possibility

Learn

We can use the words **might**, **may** or **could** to say something is possible, but not 100 % certain. We call them **modal verbs**.

Verb	Meaning	Example
may	It is quite possible.	We **may** plan a trip soon.
could	It is less possible.	We **could** plan a train trip.
might	No one is sure.	We **might** plan a trip to the moon!

We **may** visit our grandparents in the holidays.

We **could** do, but we are already quite busy.

Practise

Read the poem. Where is the modal verb?

Postcard from School Camp

Dear Mum and Dad,

Weather's poor, food's bad, teachers are grumpy, instructors are mad. Cramped in tent, cold at night, no dry clothes, boots too tight. Didn't like canoeing, the hiking was tough, all in all I've had enough.
Bye for now, MAY see you soon
If I survive this afternoon.
Your loving son,
Ben xx

P.S. Can I come again next year?

By Richard Caley

Let's talk

Discuss these questions with a partner.

1 How many things does Ben list as negative?

2 How do you know that Ben likes School Camp?

3 What do you think the afternoon activity could be?

4 What is the modal verb in the P.S. question?

Practise

1 Find the rhyming words in the poem for each of these words:

a bad

b night

c tough

d soon

2 Finish each sentence.

a I may …

b I could …

c I might …

Practise

Write a postcard from school camp.

1 Copy this poem in your notebook.

2 Change the underlined words to make it your own poem.

Dear <u>Mum and Dad</u>,

<u>Weather's</u> poor, <u>food's bad</u>, teachers are <u>grumpy</u>, instructors are mad. Cramped in <u>tent</u>, cold at night, no <u>dry clothes</u>, boots too tight. Didn't like <u>canoeing</u>, the <u>hiking</u> was tough, all in all I've had enough.
        Bye for now, <u>MAY</u> see you soon
          If I survive this afternoon.
              Your loving <u>son</u>,
                <u>Ben</u> xx

P.S. <u>Can I come again next year</u>?

Reading

Tourists in Machu Picchu

Practise

Read what Sanchia and Pia think about tourists in Machu Picchu in Peru, South America.

Sanchia's opinion

More tourists could spoil Machu Picchu.

There are plans to have a new airport built close to Machu Picchu so more people can visit, but too many tourists could spoil it. Tourists may bring litter and planes bring pollution. The site is special because it is hard to reach and it might not be so special if everyone can get there easily. Local people might not be ready for even more tourists.

Pia's opinion

We need to share beautiful places in the world.

Everyone wants to see Machu Picchu! Local people can make money from the tourists. There may be new restaurants and shops. When tourists see the site, they will see how special it is. They could learn about how important it is to protect places like Machu Picchu when they see it. They may then help us to look after it.

Hint

opinion: what someone thinks about something

Do you know?

Machu Picchu is the site of an ancient Inca city. It is high in the Andes of Peru. You can plan a trip to visit the ruins. It is a UNESCO World Heritage Site and is one of the New 7 Wonders of the World.

Practise

1 Find the words in the text.

2 Match the words to their meanings.

a ancient — people who visit countries on holiday

b ruins — to get to

c tourists — to take care of something or to look after it

d protect — dirt in the air that can spoil other things

e pollution — old buildings that are falling down

f to reach — very, very old

3 Write the words and their meanings in your notebook.

Practise

Answer the questions in your notebook.

1 What is Machu Picchu?

2 What does Sanchia think about tourists at Machu Picchu?

3 What does Pia think about tourists at Machu Picchu?

4 Do the sisters think the same?

5 What is one good thing about tourists?

6 What is one bad thing about tourists?

Let's talk

1 Work in two groups.
   • Group 1 agrees with Sanchia that more tourists could spoil Machu Picchu.
   • Group 2 agrees with Pia that we need to share beautiful places in the world

2 Take turns to speak. Share your ideas.

3 Who wins? Why?

Writing

Planning a trip

Practise

Work in a group. Plan a trip.

1 Look at the pictures and agree on where you want to visit.

2 Write a list of reasons why you might or might not visit the place.

Taj Mahal

Coral reef

Rainforest

Great Wall of China

Practise

Work together. Make a poster like this.

- Write and draw your ideas on the poster.
- Decorate your poster.

Where you are planning to visit:

Three reasons why you should not go:

1 _____
2 _____
3 _____

Three reasons why you should go:

1 _____
2 _____
3 _____

Go or don't go? What your group thinks:

Try this

1 Use your poster to share your ideas with the class.

2 Listen to others' opinions too.

Challenge yourself!

Check your poster.

- **Spelling:** Are all words spelled correctly?
- **Handwriting:** Are the letters clear?
- **Layout:** Does it look good?

Do you need to change anything to make your poster better?

What can you do?

Read and review what you can do.

- ✔ I can read, write and talk about planning a trip.
- ✔ I can use **will** to talk about plans and **could**, **may** and **might** to talk about possible plans.
- ✔ I can use **each** and **every**.
- ✔ I can read and write about feelings and different opinions.

Practise

Read the sentences. Then copy and complete them in your notebook.

(will) (going to) (been)

(always) (could) (go) (nothing) (already)

1 Banko and Jin have _____ wanted to go to the World Robot Olympiad.

2 Banko and Jin are _____ sign up this year and their dad _____ be their coach.

3 Guss and Elok have _____ planned this weekend, but they might _____ kayaking.

4 Elok has never _____ kayaking, but Guss went kayaking down a river last summer.

5 Sanchia wants to do _____ different for her birthday this year.

6 Pia suggests they _____ visit a castle, but Sanchia has _____ been to the Wulff Castle.

Try this

Look at the picture and answer the questions in your notebook.

1 Is the girl going to make a robot that walks?

2 Have the boys finished building their robots yet?

3 What might the girl's robot be able to do?

4 What can you say to offer your help?

5 Whose robot will be the best? Why?

6 Have you ever built a robot?

Practise

Write questions in your notebook for these answers.

1 Yes, she is going to climb a mountain.
2 They are going to the zoo tomorrow.
3 No, I have never been to the theatre.
4 Yes, he has always wanted to visit the Taj Mahal!
5 At the robot museum, we will learn about robots.
6 We will use a computer to build the robot.

Let's talk

Read the questions and discuss them with a partner.

1 Where are you going on your next holiday?
2 What are you going to do for your birthday this year?
3 What will you do this evening?
4 Have you ever been in a hot air balloon?
5 What have you always wanted to see?
6 Is there anything you have always wanted? Why?

Challenge yourself!

You're planning a weekend camping with your family. There are no shops, restaurants or people where you are going. Write a list of ten things in your notebook that you will take with you and say why.

Project 1

Countries of the world: Make a passport

1 Use the worksheet that your teacher will give you.

- Fill in the missing words.

- Draw a picture of yourself for your passport.

- Fill in the visas (the countries you have visited and the countries you still want to visit).

PASSPORT

VISAS

Name
Date of birth
Birthplace
Nationality
Special features
Signed

2 Work with a partner. Choose a country you want to visit.

- Research the country.

- What money is used there?

- Which language is spoken there?

- Find five places of interest to visit.

3 Work with a partner. Choose a country that you want to visit.

- Show your passport.

- Role play being a tourist and visiting two places of interest in your country.

Project 2

Let's feast

1 Use the worksheet that your teacher will give you.

- Think of which foods you would like to show on your menu. Use this list to help you.

  - Starters

  - Main course

  - Desserts

  - Drinks

- Fill in your menu.

2 Work with a partner.

- Make a list of all the ingredients you will need.

- Make a list of other things you will need, such as:

  - decorations

  - music

  - cutlery and crockery.

3 In a small group, role-play hosting a party in your house.

- Talk to your friends, and offer them food and drinks.

- Let them choose off your menu.

Project 3

Make a model home

1 Make a model home. You can make your home from ice-cream sticks, cardboard or paper.

Ice-cream stick house

Cardboard house

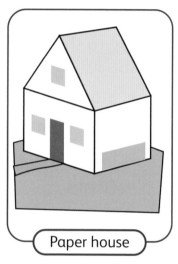

Paper house

2 Show your partner your house.

- Describe your house.
- Tell them about the special features of your house.

3 Work in small groups.

- Put all your houses together to make a street or a neighbourhood.
- Add other features, such as parks, libraries or special areas just for children.

You will need:

- building materials of your choice, such as paper, cardboard, ice-cream sticks, lego blocks
- decorations
- crayons or paint
- a sturdy base

Project 4

How does the sun orbit the Earth?

1 Make a model of how the sun orbits the Earth.

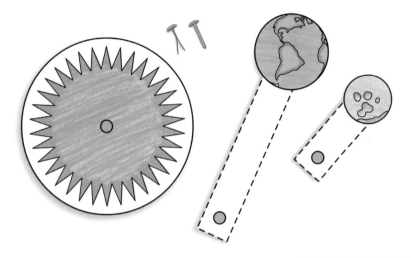

You will need:

- the worksheet that your teacher will give you
- scissors
- glue
- crayons or pencil crayons
- split pins

Instructions:

- Paste the worksheet onto a piece of card.
- Colour in the sun, moon and Earth.
- Cut out along the dotted lines.
- Make a tiny hole in the center of the Earth.
- Insert the split pin.
- Add the arm of the moon to the same split pin.
- Use the second split pin to attach the sun to the arm of the Earth.
- Practise moving the moon around the Earth and the Earth around the sun.

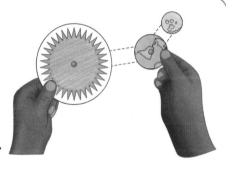

2 With a partner, talk about how the Earth moves around the sun and how the moon moves around the Earth. Use your model to explain the processes to each other.

3 In small groups, take turns to be the sun, the moon or the Earth and to role-play moving around each other. Choose a volunteer to do the explaining. Share your role play with other groups or the class.

Project 5

Festival of music

1 Make an instrument.

- Use your imagination and make an instrument from recycled materials. Look at the pictures for inspiration.

- Play your own instrument.

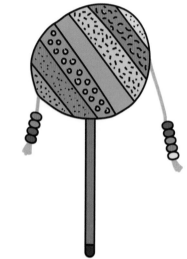

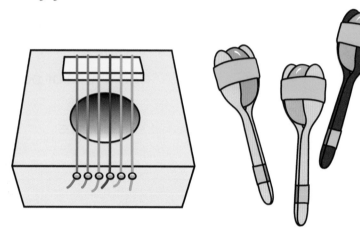

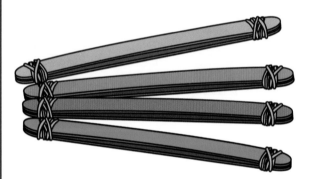

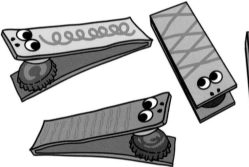

2 With your partner, make up a song or set a well-known rhyme to music using your musical instruments.

3 Work in small groups. Create your own music festival with each individual or pair taking turns to play their song or rhyme set to music. Share your festival with the rest of the class.

Project 6

Tales from the past

1 Write a comic strip.

- Use the worksheet that your teacher will give you.
- Think of a story from your family history.
- First, draw pictures to tell the story.
- Then add the words.
- Use the speech bubbles and add some speech bubbles of your own.

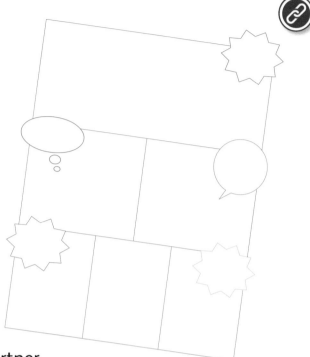

2 Share your comic strip with your partner.

- Take turns to read each other's stories.
- Say one thing that you like about your partner's story.
- Say one thing that your partner can change.

3 Share your stories with your group.

- Make a group book of all the stories.
- Swap the books with the rest of the class.

Project 7

Make a robot hand

1 Make a robot hand.

You will need:

- tape
- scissors
- cardboard
- drinking straws
- wider straws
- wool or string (different colours if possible)

Instructions:

- Draw around your hand on the piece of cardboard.
- Cut out the hand (picture 1).
- Draw your finger joints on the cardboard hand (picture 2).

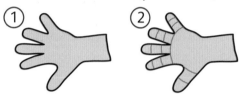

- Fold along the lines (picture 3).

- Cut the smaller straws to fit along the fingers, leaving gaps into pieces to thread the string.

- Paste the pieces of straw onto the hand.
- Paste a wider piece of straw onto the wrist part of the hand.
- Thread the string through the straws. Use a different colour for each finger if possible.
- Each finger must have its own string.
- Thread all five of the strings through the bigger straw.

2 Work with your partner and practise moving your robotic hands.

3 In groups, play a game.

- Put a whole pile of different objects in the middle of the circle.
- See who can pick up the most objects with their robotic hands.
- Try to pick up objects of different sizes.
- Discuss which objects are easier to pick up. Say why.
- Can you think of an easier way to make your robotic hand move?

Project 8

Adventures

1 Use the worksheet that your teacher will give you and follow the instructions to make a kite.

You will need:

- A4 piece of card
- wooden skewer or straw
- kite string or fishing line
- ribbon or colourful plastic strips
- scissors or a hole punch
- tape

2 Compare kites with a partner. What is the same and what is different?

3 If your teacher agrees, go outside in small groups to fly your kites.

- Whose kite flew the highest?
- Whose kite stayed in the air the longest?
- Whose kite couldn't fly? Can you think of a reason why?

Project 9

Planning a trip

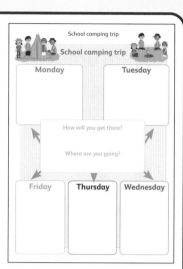

1 Think of your favourite activities for a school camp. Write them down.

2 Tell your partner about some activities that you would like to do on a school camp. If you have the same ideas, think of something different.

3 Work in small groups. Use the writing template that your teacher will give you and make an activity list.

- Include two activities per day.

- Write what you would need for each activity.

- Share your school camp ideas with the rest of the class.

Glossary of grammar

Unit 1

Infinitive of purpose

We use the **infinitive of purpose** to say why we do something.

- I went to Spain **to learn** Spanish.
- I went to the beach **to enjoy** the sea.
- I went to the shops **to buy** ice cream.

Gerunds

A **gerund** is a verb used as a noun. It is an action being used as a thing or idea.

- I love **swimming** in the lake.
- They went **sightseeing**.

Past simple tense

We use the past simple tense to talk about something that happened in the past.

- We **went** to the UK.
- We **flew** in a plane.
- We **stayed** in a hotel.

Time connectives

Time connectives tell us when something is happening or when it happened.

- We fastened our seatbelts **before** the plane took off.
- On a long trip, people sleep **after** they have eaten a meal.
- Travellers can relax **when** the plane is in the air.
- The pilot tells everyone to prepare for landing, **then** he lands the plane.

Unit 2

Countable and uncountable nouns

Countable nouns are things we can count, for example, a large egg, a cup or a spoon.

Uncountable nouns are things we can't count, for example, some milk, some flour, some oil.

Offering: *Would you like …?*

When we offer somebody something, we can say: **Would you like …?**

- Would **you like** a pancake?
- Would **you like** some honey?

Quantifiers: *a few, few, a little, little*

We use **quantifiers** to talk about the **number** or **amount** of something. We can use **a few**, **few**, **a little** and **little** to talk about small numbers and amounts.

- There are **a few** tasty ones over there.
- There are **few** snack choices today.
- I will share **a little** of my water.
- We have **little** money.

Inviting: *Would you like to…?*

When we want to invite somebody to do something, we ask: **Would you like to …?**

- **Would you like to** have a picnic?
- **Would you like to** eat a snack?

Unit 3

Imperatives

We use the **imperative** form of the verb for instructions and commands.
- **Tell** me who lives here.
- **Don't go** up the stairs! **Stop**!

Prepositions of direction: *into, out of, from, towards*

We use some prepositions to talk about the direction things are moving in: **into, out of, from, towards**.
- He looked **into** the window.
- He looked **out of** the window.
- He ran **from** the house.
- He ran **towards** the house.

Question tags

We can use a **question tag** to turn a statement into a question and to check what we think we know is true.
- The bears are out, **aren't they?**
- You know that story, **don't you?**

Unit 4

Present continuous tense for the future

We use the **present continuous tense** to talk about what people are doing. We can also use the **present continuous** to talk about plans we have made for the future.
- **I'm staying** up late this evening to see the full moon.
- **I'm inviting** some friends here to watch it with us.

Verbs with to infinitive

We use **verbs with to + infinitive** to talk about what something is for.
I use my sketchbook and pencil **to draw** the moon and the stars.

Have to and don't have to

We use **have to** when we must do something, and **don't have to** when we don't need to do something.
- Space explorers **have to** wear spacesuits in space.
- Space explorers **don't have to** travel alone.

Adjectives for comparing

We use **comparatives** to compare things and **superlatives** to say which thing is top in a group.
- The sun is a million times **bigger** than the Earth.
- The sun is the **closest** star to Earth.

For regular words:

	add er / est	drop y, add ier / iest	add more / the most
adjective	bright	shiny	interesting
comparative	brighter	shinier	more interesting
superlative	the brightest	the shiniest	the most interesting

Don't forget the irregular words: **many or much, more, the most, and little, less, the least!**

Unit 5

Present simple tense

We use the **present simple tense** to talk about: **routines**, which are things we do often and at the same time; **habits**, which are things we often or always do; and **states**, which are our opinions, our senses and how we feel.

- I **have** piano lessons on Wednesdays.
- He **plays** it well.
- I **love** my new earphones.

Gerunds

We use **gerunds** when we want to talk about what we **like doing** or **don't like doing**.

- Super Sita **enjoys playing** the piano.
- I **don't like playing** the trumpet.

Defining relative clauses

We use **defining relative clauses** to add information about people, places and things to a sentence: **who, which, that, where.**

- Elvis Presley is the singer **who** is called 'King of Rock and Roll'.
- This is the guitar **which/that** Elvis first played.
- Mississippi is the town **where** Elvis grew up.

Adverbs for comparing

We use **comparative adverbs** to compare things and **superlative adverbs** to say which thing is top in a group.

- I think you are singing **more loudly** now.
- I think you sing **more loudly than** me.
- Yes! I sing **the loudest** in my class.

For regular words:

adverbs	loudly	beautifully
comparative	more loudly less loudly	more beautifully less beautifully
superlative	the loudest the least loudest	the most beautifully the least beautifully

Don't forget the irregular words: **good, well, better than, the best, and bad, badly, worse than, the worst**!

Unit 6

Subordinate clauses

We use a **subordinate clause** to tell us more about the past, starting with: **when, before, after**.

- I like to read stories **before** I go to bed.
- I enjoy reading legends **when** one animal tricks another.
- I looked at the pictures **after** I read the story.

Past continuous tense

We use the **past continuous tense** to talk about what people were doing in the past.

- Maui **was hiding** in the fishing canoe as his brothers rowed it out to sea.
- He **was waiting** to jump out and surprise his brothers.

Descriptions with *like*

We can use **like** to talk about things we enjoy, and **look like** to talk about how something looks.

- I **liked** the story of the *Great Hunter*.
- The prince **looked like** an impala.

Had to and *didn't have to*

We use **had to** when there was an obligation to do something in the past, and **didn't have to** when there was no obligation to do something in the past.

- Sang Kancil **had to** think quickly to trick Tiger.
- Tiger **didn't have to** believe Sang Kancil.

Unit 7

Be going to for plans

We can use **be going to** when we talk about plans that we have already decided on.

- I know our robot is the best. I'm **going to** look at the other robots.
- **Are** you **going to** build the robot's arms next? Yes, we **are**.

Something, nothing, anything

We can use **something**, **nothing** and **anything** as **pronouns** and to give an idea of how much we are talking about.

- That team is building **something** special.
- Can I help with **anything**?
- I can't find **anything** wrong with it.
- **Nothing** was happening.
- There is **nothing** to show.

Unit 8

Present perfect tense: *Have you ever …?*

We use the **present perfect tense** to talk about something that started in the past and is still happening. We use it with **ever** to talk about our experiences.

- **I have climbed** to the top of a climbing wall.
- **Have** you **ever climbed** a mountain?
- No, **I've never** climbed a mountain.

Adverbs to use with the present perfect tense: *never, yet, already, always*

We can use the adverbs **never, yet, already** and **always** to talk about the time of any action: **how often** and **when**.

- I have **never** sailed a boat.
- I've ridden a camel, but I haven't ridden an elephant **yet**.
- I've **always** wanted to camp in the jungle.
- I have **already** learned how to ride a mountain bike.

Unit 9

Future simple tense: *will*

We use **will** to talk about the future. We can use it to predict, to mean the same as the word 'want', and to make or talk about a promise.

- Do you think you **will** stay away for one or two nights?
- **Will** everyone be allowed to go?
- Yes, they **will**.

Determiners: *each, every*

We use **each** to talk about things or people in a group one at a time, and **every** to talk about the whole group.

- In **every** group, there will be a leader.
- Students will look after **each** other too.

Might, may, could for possibility

We use **might**, **may** and **could** to say something is possible.

- We **may** visit our grandparents in the holidays.
- We **could** do, but we are already quite busy.
- We **might** plan a trip to the moon.

Vocabulary

adventures

apartment

batteries

beams

bionic (arm)

bookmark

brass band

camping

canoe

castle

chicken

chimney

coach (a person, not a vehicle)

coconut

compass

competition

coral reef

cottage

couches

crocodile

cushions

cycling

desert

door

drums

Earth

e-book

eclipse

eggs

elephant

family

festival

fish

fishing

flute

football stadium

footprint

frying pan

geocaching

gong

guitar

hiking

home

honey

house

impala

International Space Station (ISS)

island

jazz band

kayaking

kitchen

LED lights

lemon slice

lion

litter

menu

moon

museum

newspaper

ocean

orienteering

pancakes

peanuts

piano

picnic

plane

planet

pollution

rainforest

restaurants

rhino

river

robot

rock

rock climbing

rocket

roof

sailor

shops

singing

snake

space explorer

springs

star

storm

strawberry jam

street food

string quartet

sugar

sun

swimming

telescope

tent

theatre

tickbird

tiger

tourists

treasure

underwater

vegetarian

village

wall

warehouse

waves

wheels

windows

world map

Acknowledgements

The Publishers would like to thank the following for permission to reproduce copyright material. Every effort has been made to trace or contact all copyright holders, but if any have been inadvertently overlooked the Publishers will be pleased to make the necessary arrangements at the first opportunity.

Text acknowledgements

p. 23 The poem 'Peace and Pancakes' © *Peace and Pancakes* by Adrian Mitchell. © Adrian Mitchell. Reproduced by kind permission of United Agents LLP; **pp. 30, 88** Extract/Cover © from *A Roman Banquet* (ISBN 9781510453739), written by Hawys Morgan, from Rising Stars Reading Planet – Level 3: Venus/Brown band; **pp. 40–41** Extract/cover/illustrations from © *Goldilocks and the Three Bears* (ISBN 9781471898716), written by Abigail Flint, from Rising Stars Reading Planet – Level 3: Galaxy/Yellow band; **pp. 54, 88** Illustration/Cover from © True Space Adventures (ISBN 9781510452329), written by Paul Shipton and illustrated by Richard Watson (Bright Group International), from Rising Stars Reading Planet – Level 1: Stars/Lime band; **pp. 67, 88** Adaption/Cover from © *Game Changers: Music-Makers* (ISBN 9781510451476), written by Ciaran Murtagh, from Rising Stars Reading Planet KS2 – Level 1; **p. 80** © *The Great Hunter*, adapted from *African Tales: A Barefoot Collection*, and used by permission of Barefoot Books, Inc. Text copyright © 2009 by Gcina Mhlophe. Illustrations copyright © 2009 by Rachel Griffin. The moral rights of Gcina Mhlophe and Rachel Griffin have been asserted; **pp. 84–86** © *Running Rhino* (African Animal Tales), Mwenye Hadithi and illustrator Adrienne Kennaway, reproduced by permission of Hodder Children's Books, an imprint of Hachette Children's Books, Carmelite House, 50 Victoria Embankment, London imprint, EC4Y 0DZ; **pp. 94–95** Extract/cover from © *World of Robots: Wild Robots* (ISBN 9781510444287), written by Joe Craig, from Rising Stars Reading Planet – Level 2: Mercury/Brown band; **p. 95** Cover from © *World of Robots: Breakdown* (ISBN 9781510444461), written by Joe Craig, from Rising Stars Reading Planet – Level 3: Venus/Brown band; **p. 95** Cover from © *World of Robots: Hijack* (ISBN 9781510444645), written by Joe Craig, from Rising Stars Reading Planet – Level 4: Earth/Grey band; **p. 97** Permission granted by © World Robot Olympiad Association Ltd; **p. 98** © *The Week Junior*/ Dennis Publishing Ltd 2020; **p. 110** The poster '50 things to do before you're 11¾' © These digital images are the property of National Trust images and are protected by copyright. All images are supplied under our terms and conditions which can be found on our website at http://www.nationaltrustimages.org.uk/pages/terms-and-conditions; **p. 120** The poem 'Dear Mum and Dad' © Richard Caley.

p. 93 This image is not an actual representation of Freddie Cook.

Photo acknowledgements

p. 5 *cc*, **p. 23** *bl* © Paul Brighton/Adobe Stock Photo; **p. 5** *cc*, **p. 23** *cc* © Circleps/Adobe Stock Photo; **p. 5** *cc*, **p. 23** *c1* © Chandler Vid 85/ Adobe Stock Photo; **p. 5** *cc*, **p. 23** *cc* © Minhyoung/Adobe Stock Photo; **p. 5** *cc*, **p. 23** *cc* © Daniel Wiedemann/Adobe Stock Photo; **p. 5** *cc*, **p. 23** *cc* © F Kruger/Adobe Stock Photo; **p. 5** *cc*, **p. 23** *cr* © Moving Moment/Adobe Stock Photo; **p. 5** *cc*, **p. 23** *bl* © Indian Style/Shutterstock Photo; **p. 5** *cc*, **p. 23** *bc* © Elena/Adobe Stock Photo; **p. 5** *cc*, **p. 23** *bc* © Nelea Reazanteva/Adobe Stock Photo; **p. 5** *cc*, **p. 23** *br* © Joanna Tkaczuk/Adobe Stock Photo; **p. 14** *br* © LM Spencer/Adobe Stock Photo; **p. 15** *tl* © Maksim B/Shutterstock Photo; **p. 15** *tr* © Zoltan Major/ Shutterstock Photo; **p. 15** *cl* © Tito Noverian Putra/EyeEm/Adobe Stock Photo; **p. 15** *cr* © Anton Ivanov/Shutterstock Photo; **p. 16** *br* © 06 Photo/Adobe Stock Photo; **p. 19** *t* © Claudia Silva Aguad/Shutterstock Photo; **p. 20** *cl* © Quick Shooting/Adobe Stock Photo; **p. 20** *cr* © Paul Hampton/Adobe Stock Photo; **p. 20** *bl* © Susan/Adobe Stock Photo; **p. 20** *br* ©Wang/Adobe Stock Photo; **p. 24** *cl* © M Studio/Adobe Stock Photo; **p. 26** *cl* © Joe Zachs from Pune, India, CC BY 2.0, via Wikimedia Common; **p. 31** *tr* © Lebrecht Music & Arts/Alamy Stock Photo; **p. 38** *bl* © Pannarai/Adobe Stock Photo; **p. 38** *br* © Дарья Колпакова/Adobe Stock Photo; **p. 39** *tr* © Idgeeva Alena/Shutterstock Photo; **p. 39** *bl* © Pachal Letnettip/Shutterstock Photo; **p. 39** *br* © Iconic Bestiary/Shutterstock Photo; **p. 46** *br* © Motortion/Adobe Stock Photo; **p. 47** *br* © Rolff Images/Adobe Stock Photo; **p. 48** *cc* © Glad Cov/Shutterstock Photo; **p. 50** *cr* © Piai/Adobe Stock Photo; **p. 50** *br* © Magdal 3na/Adobe Stock Photo; **p. 51** *cl* © Solar Seven/Shutterstock Photo; **p. 51** *cr* © Paulista/Adobe Stock Photo; **p. 51** *cc* © Nerthuz/Shutterstock Photo; **p. 51** *bl* © Bogdan Syrotynskyi/Shutterstock Photo; **p. 52** *cl* © Granger Historical Picture Archive/Alamy Stock Photo; **p. 52** *cc* © Pictorial Press Ltd/Alamy Stock Photo; **p. 52** *cc* © NASA Photo/Alamy Stock Photo; **p. 52** *cc* © Art Directors & TRIP/Alamy Stock Photo; **p. 52** *cr* © GL Archive/Alamy Stock Photo; **p. 53** *t* © 3000ad/Shutterstock; **p. 53** *bl* © Hachette UK; **p. 55** *b* © PeamDesign/Shutterstock Photo; **p. 63** *tr* © Fashion Stock.com/Shutterstock Photo; **p. 63** *br* © IR Stone/Adobe Stock Photo; **p. 64** *tr* © High Way Starz/Adobe Stock Photo; **p. 64** *bl* © Tiler 84/Adobe Stock Photo; **p. 64** *bc* © Elena Schweitzer/Adobe Stock Photo; **p. 64** *bc* © Small Tom/Adobe Stock Photo; **p. 64** *br* © Direk Takmatcha/Adobe Stock Photo; **p. 67** *cr* © Pictorial Press Ltd/Alamy Stock Photo; **p. 68** *tr* © Michael Ochs Archives/Stringer/ Getty Images; **p. 69** *tl* © RB/Staff/Getty Images; **p. 69** *tr* © Fotan/Alamy Stock Photo; **p. 69** *cl* © Cynthia Johnson/Contributor/Getty Images; **p. 69** *cr* © Adrian Dennis/Staff/Getty Images; **p. 70** *br* © Cherry and Bees/Adobe Stock Photo; **p. 74** *cl* © Valentyna/Adobe Stock Photo; **p. 74** *cc* © Екатерина Зирина/Adobe Stock Photo; **p. 74** *cr* © Valentyna/Adobe Stock Photo; **p. 78** *b* © Beelaa/Adobe Stock Photo; **p. 85** *br* © Thomas Amby/Adobe Stock Photo; **p. 86** *br* © Wave Break Media Micro/Adobe Stock Photo; **p. 88** *tr* © Wave Break Media Micro/ Adobe Stock Photo; **p. 97** *tr* © Anadolu Agency/Contributor/Getty Images; **p. 97** *cl* © Anadolu Agency/Contributor/Getty Images; **p. 97** *cr* © Hindustan Times/Contributor/Getty Images; **p. 97** *br* © Martynova Anna/Shutterstock Photo; **p. 101** *tr* © Andrew Walmsley/Alamy Stock Photo; **p. 103** *br* © DPA Picture Alliance/Alamy Stock Photo; **p. 104** *cc* © Max Topchii/Adobe Stock Photo; **p. 104** *cr*, **p. 108** *bl* © Brocreative/Adobe Stock Photo; **p. 105** *br* © Reisegraf/Adobe Stock Photo; **p. 106** *cr* © Phil Fisk/Guardian/Eyevine.; **p. 107** *tr* © Phil Fisk/ Guardian/Eyevine.; **p. 108** *bc* © Phil Fisk/Guardian/Eyevine.; **p. 109** *br* © Kobchai M/Adobe Stock Photo; **p. 111** *cl* © Ansyvan/Adobe Stock Photo; **p. 111** *bl* © Sarah/Adobe Stock Photo; **p. 116** *cr* © Janista/Adobe Stock Photo; **p. 117** *cr* © Angelov/Adobe Stock Photo; **p. 117** *br* © Godfer/Adobe Stock Photo; **p. 118** *bc* © Colport/Alamy Stock Photo; **p. 120** *cr* © 313 Design/Shutterstock Photo; **p. 121** *cr* © 313 Design/ Shutterstock Photo; **p. 122** *bl* © Saiko 3p/Adobe Stock Photo; **p. 122** *br* © Daniel Prudek/Adobe Stock Photo; **p. 123** *tl* © Adwo/Adobe Stock Photo; **p. 124** *tl* © Refresh (PIX)/Adobe Stock Photo; **p. 124** *tr* © John Anderson/Adobe Stock Photo; **p. 124** *bl* © Simon/Adobe Stock Photo; **p. 124** *br* © Zhao Jiankang/Adobe Stock Photo; **p. 126** *br* © Yuriy Golub/Shutterstock Photo; **p. 127** *b* © Olga Danylenko/Shutterstock Photo; **p. 128** *cl* © Rawf 8/Adobe Stock Photo; **p. 128** *br* © Tom Wang/Adobe Stock Photo; **p. 129** *cc*, *cc* © Tartila/Adobe Stock Photo; **p. 129** *cc* © Tartila/Shutterstock Photo; **p. 129** *cc* © Catalyst Labs/Shutterstock Photo; **p. 129** *cc* © N Azlin Sha/Shutterstock Photo; **p. 129** *cr* © Sergii Moscaliuk/Adobe Stock Photo; **p. 129** *br* © Wavebreak Media Micro/Adobe Stock Photo; **p. 132** *br* © Yoshi 5/Shutterstock.com; **p. 135** *br* © Andrey Apoev/Adobe Stock Photo.

t = top, *b* = bottom, *l* = left, *r* = right, *c* = centre